AMERICAN MONUMENT

AMERICAN MONUMENT

LYNN DAVIS

INTRODUCTION BY *WITOLD* RYBCZYNSKI

THE MONACELLI PRESS

First published in the United States of America in 2004 by
The Monacelli Press, Inc.
902 Broadway, New York, New York 10010.

Library of Congress Cataloging-in-Publication Data
Davis, Lynn, 1944–
American monument / Lynn Davis ; introduction by Witold Rybczynski.
p. cm.
ISBN 1-58093-149-9
1. Architectural photography—United States. 2. Monuments—United States—Pictorial works. 3. Davis, Lynn, 1944– . I. Title.
TR659.D385 2004
779'.473'092—dc22 2004054670

Printed and bound in Italy

Designed by Evan Schoninger

Credits
page 81: Donald Judd, 15 *Untitled Works in Concrete* (detail), 1980–84, art © Judd Foundation, Licensed by VAGA, New York, New York
page 147: Dan Flavin, *Untitled* (an installation of two sets of two eight -foot, two-lamp fixtures mounted diagonally on each angled foyer wall of Richmond Hall), 1996, daylight flourescent light, each set: 124.0 by 153.5 by 4.8 inches, The Menil Collection, Huston, Texas, © 2004 Estate of Dan Flavin/Artists Right Society (ARS), New York, New York

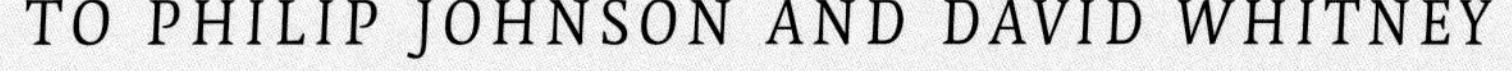

TO PHILIP JOHNSON AND DAVID WHITNEY

REALLY, REALLY BIG

WITOLD RYBCZYNSKI

Americans have never trodden lightly on the land. We want to leave our mark. But we don't simply scratch hieroglyphs on a rock face or raise a cairn; we build a transcontinental railroad, an interstate highway system, a Hoover Dam. We are not shy. When we erect a missile silo in a cornfield, it assumes the mythic grandeur of a Mayan pyramid. Sometimes we reshape the entire landscape in our image. There is nothing more spectacular, more monstrous—and more truly American—than Mount Rushmore.

In some ways, the American drive to build monuments resembles the ancient Roman attraction to great works of engineering. There is the same need to impose order, to subjugate, to compel. And just as the grandest Roman monuments were fundamentally utilitarian—aqueducts, arenas, and public baths—the grandest American monuments are dams, bridges, and lighthouses. Americans are never as majestically monumental as when they are intently practical. One of the most affecting monuments I have ever seen was a windmill farm in California. Dozens of tall masts with rotating propellers made me think less of a public utility than of a collection of children's whirligigs blown up to Brobdingnagian proportions. For a commercial, materialistic nation that is supposedly obsessed by the bottom line, we seem to delight in needless bigness. Higher, longer, larger are irresistible calls. We can't help ourselves.

Even the most venal billboard, the gaudiest neon sign, is a kind of monument. Standing forlornly beside the road or sticking out above the treetops, it is a reminder that in a democracy, anyone can be a monument builder. *If someone was able to do this*, they insinuate, *think what you could do.*

No one would call the Washington Monument a billboard. L'Enfant's original plan for the city had imagined an equestrian statue of the first president; fifty years later John Mills proposed an Egyptian obelisk instead. That was not, in itself, original. What was distinctively American about the design was its unprecedented size. The largest obelisk at the time, in the piazza of St. John Lateran in Rome, was just under 106 feet tall. The tip of the Washington Monument is more than 550 feet in the air.

When you stand at the base of this colossal granite shaft, you realize that it is not a monument sized for the Mall, or even for the city; it is intended for the entire continent. Monuments seem to suit America's immense scale. It has something to do with the landscape: the great inland lakes, the prairies, the western deserts. Nature itself is so vast that it is a challenge, a dare to be commensurately grand. The first inhabitants of North America felt this call. The Iroquois constructed immense longhouses occupied by as many as four hundred people. The twelfth-century Mississippian culture built Cahokia, a great city characterized by giant earthworks. At Chaco Canyon, the Anasazi of the Southwest erected a number of so-called Great Houses, monumental complexes of plazas, towers, and terraces. And some of the most impressive indigenous buildings are the extraordinary decorated plank houses built by the Kwakiutl and the Haida on the northwest coast of the Pacific.

The most characteristic feature of the plank house is the frontal pole, or totem, carved with images of animals, make-believe beasts, and humans. These structures were both aesthetic and mythical. That modern American totem, the skyscraper, likewise has a magical dimension. It is ostensibly utilitarian, a place where people live or work, yet its prime function is symbolic. More than streets and squares, it represents the American city. It is a curiously ephemeral symbol: unreachable, untouchable, distant.

It may be a sense of insecurity that has caused us to think at such a large scale. After all, compared to the slow majesty of the Mississippi, the plunge of Niagara, the silent expanse of the Great Plains, or the towering rise of redwood groves, most man-made structures seem temporary, in danger of being swept away—by the weather, by catastrophe, or merely by the course of time. So we overcompensate. We make our monuments big. Really, really big.

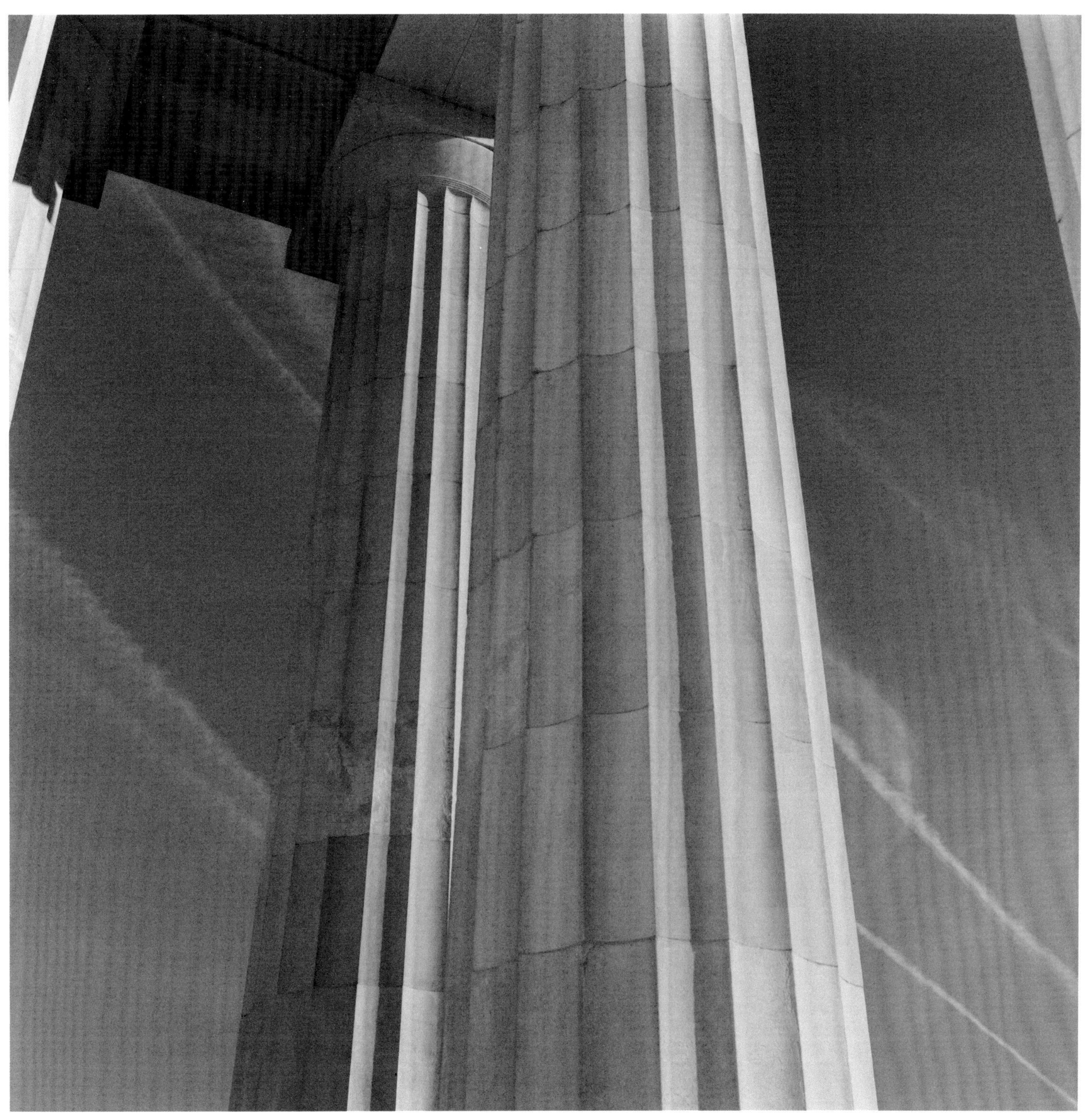

Lincoln Memorial
Henry Bacon, 1911–22 • Washington, D.C.

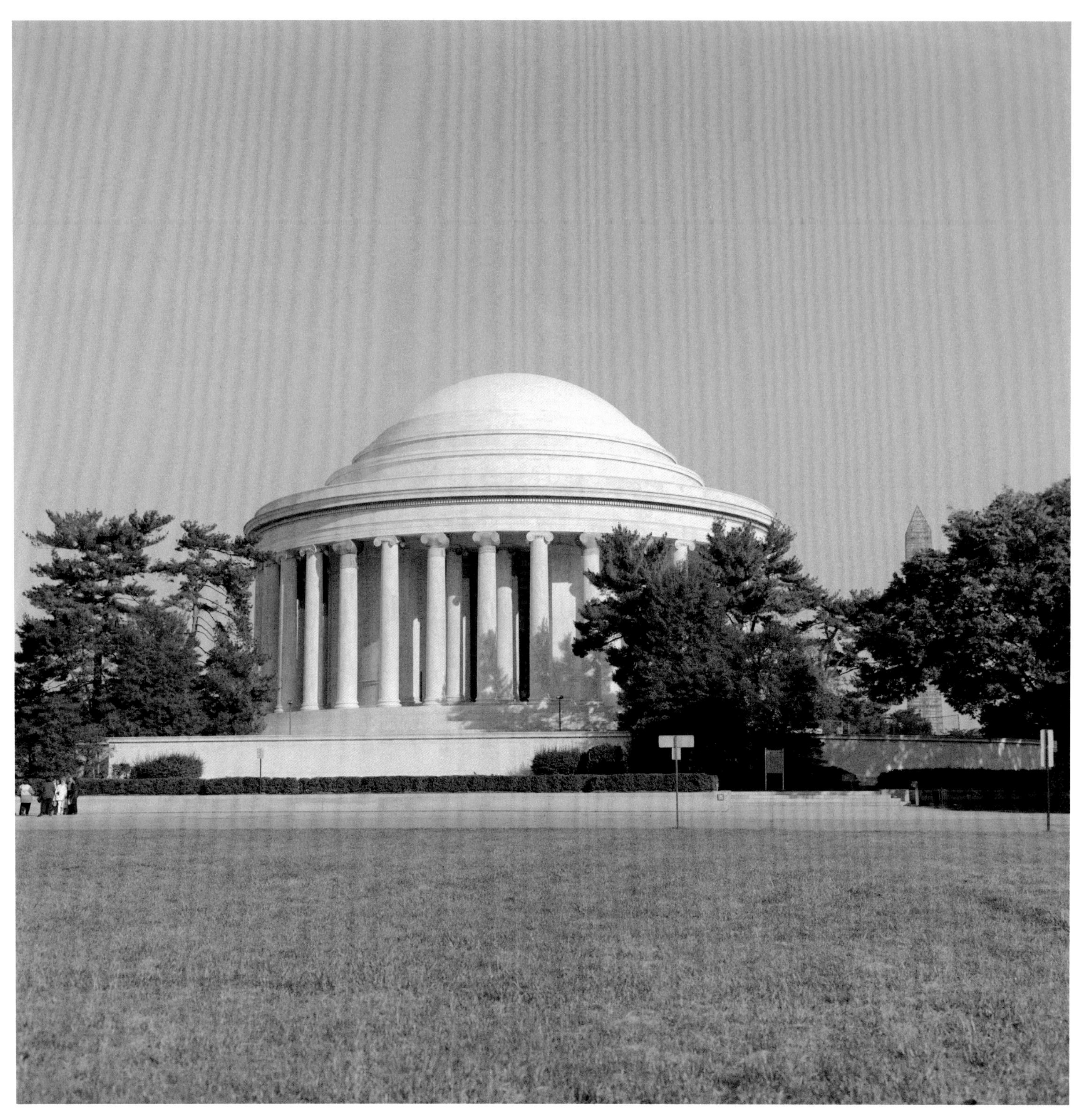

Jefferson Monument
John Russell Pope, 1937–43 • Washington, D.C.

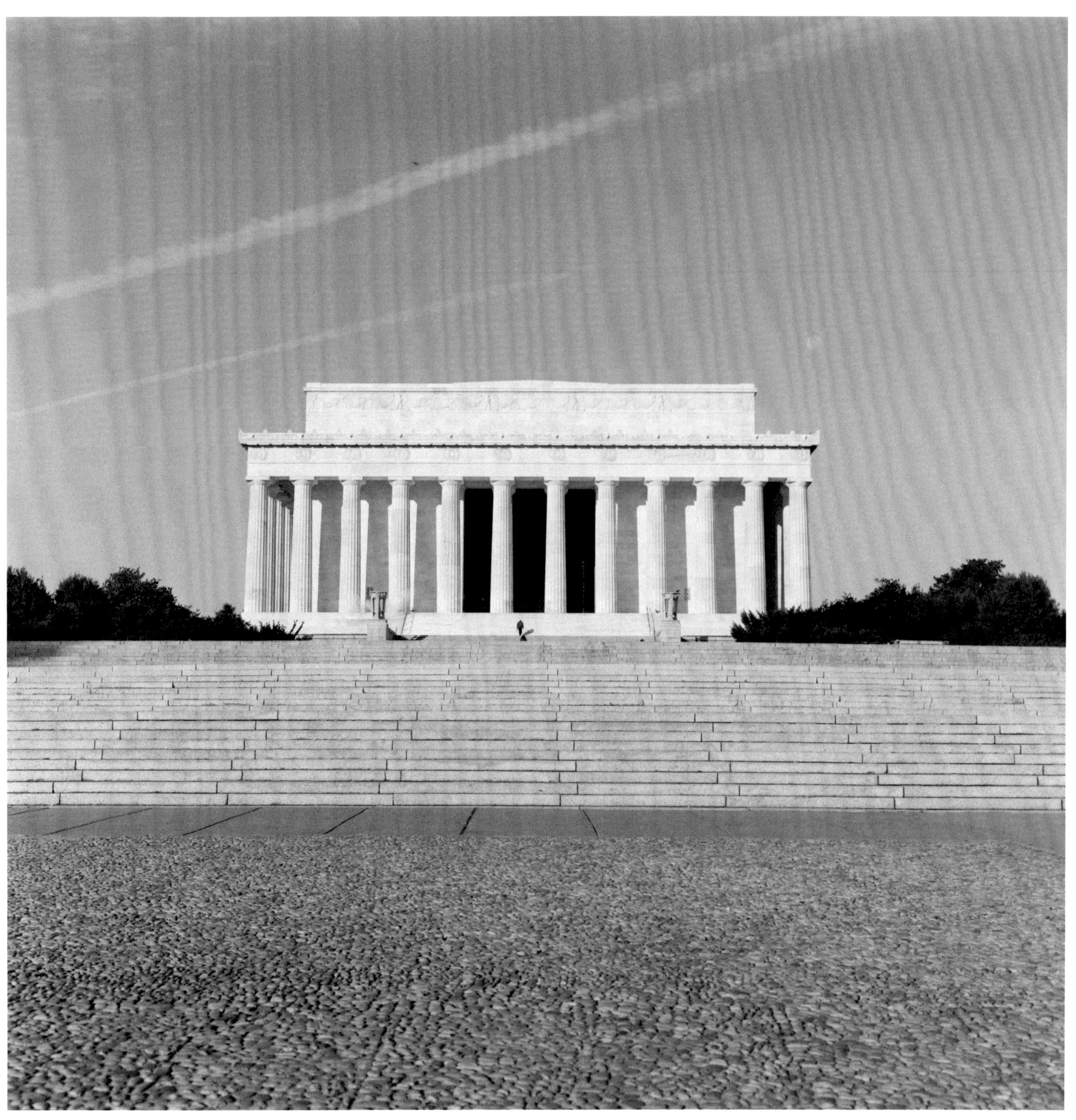

Lincoln Memorial
Henry Bacon, 1911–22 • Washington, D.C.

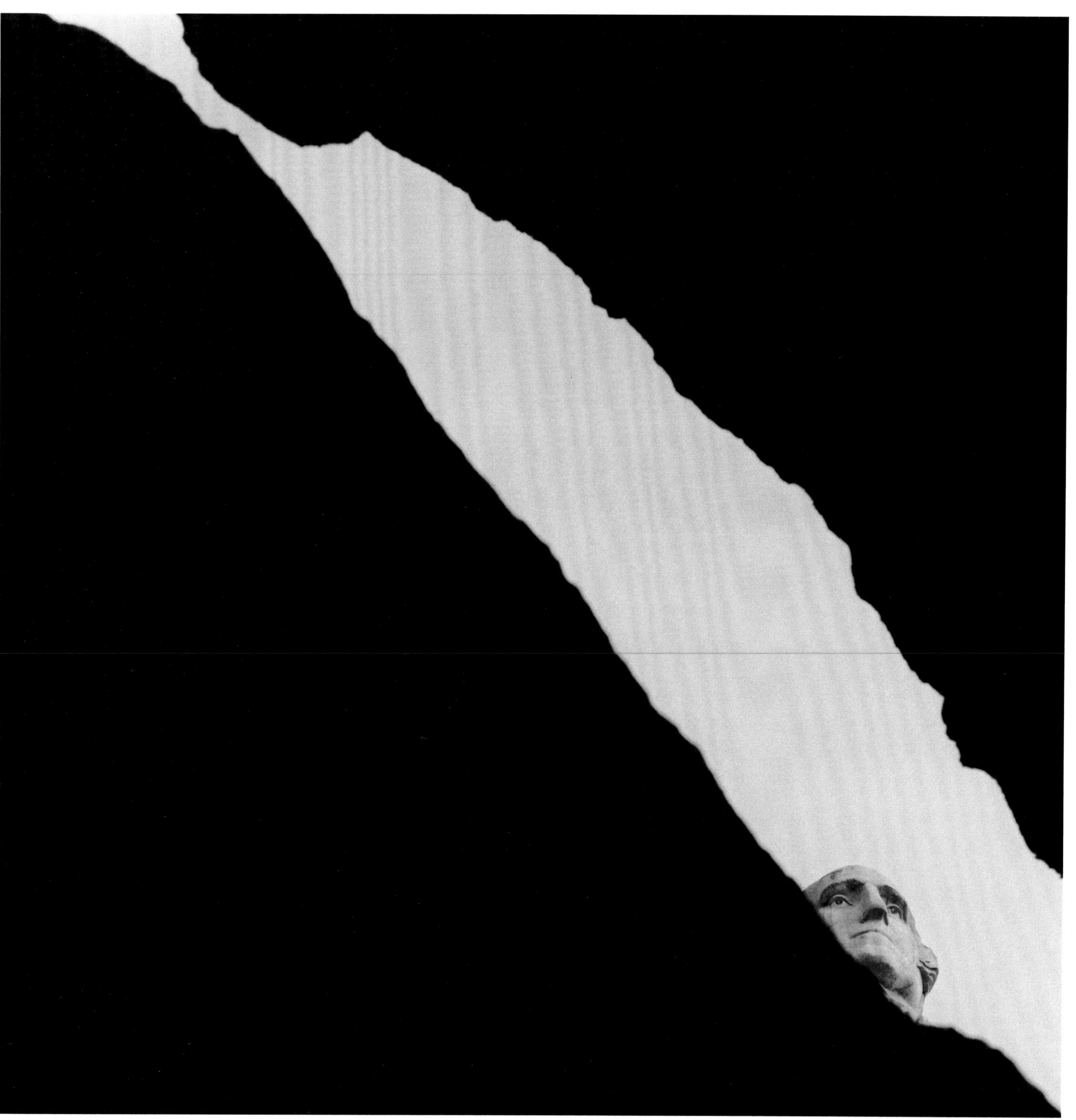

Mount Rushmore
Gutzon Borglum, 1927–41 • Black Hills National Forest, South Dakota

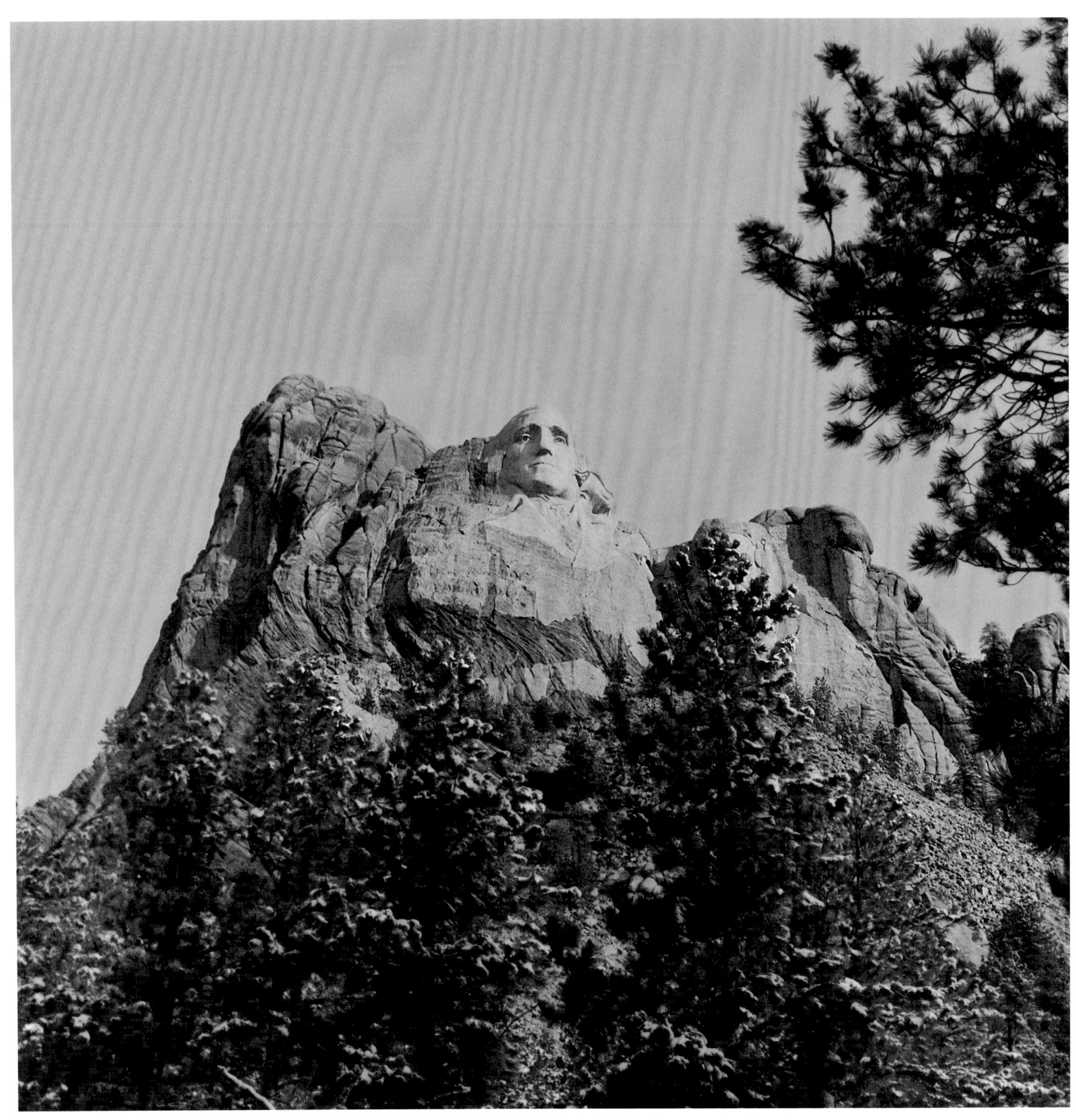

Mount Rushmore
Gutzon Borglum, 1927–41 • Black Hills National Forest, South Dakota

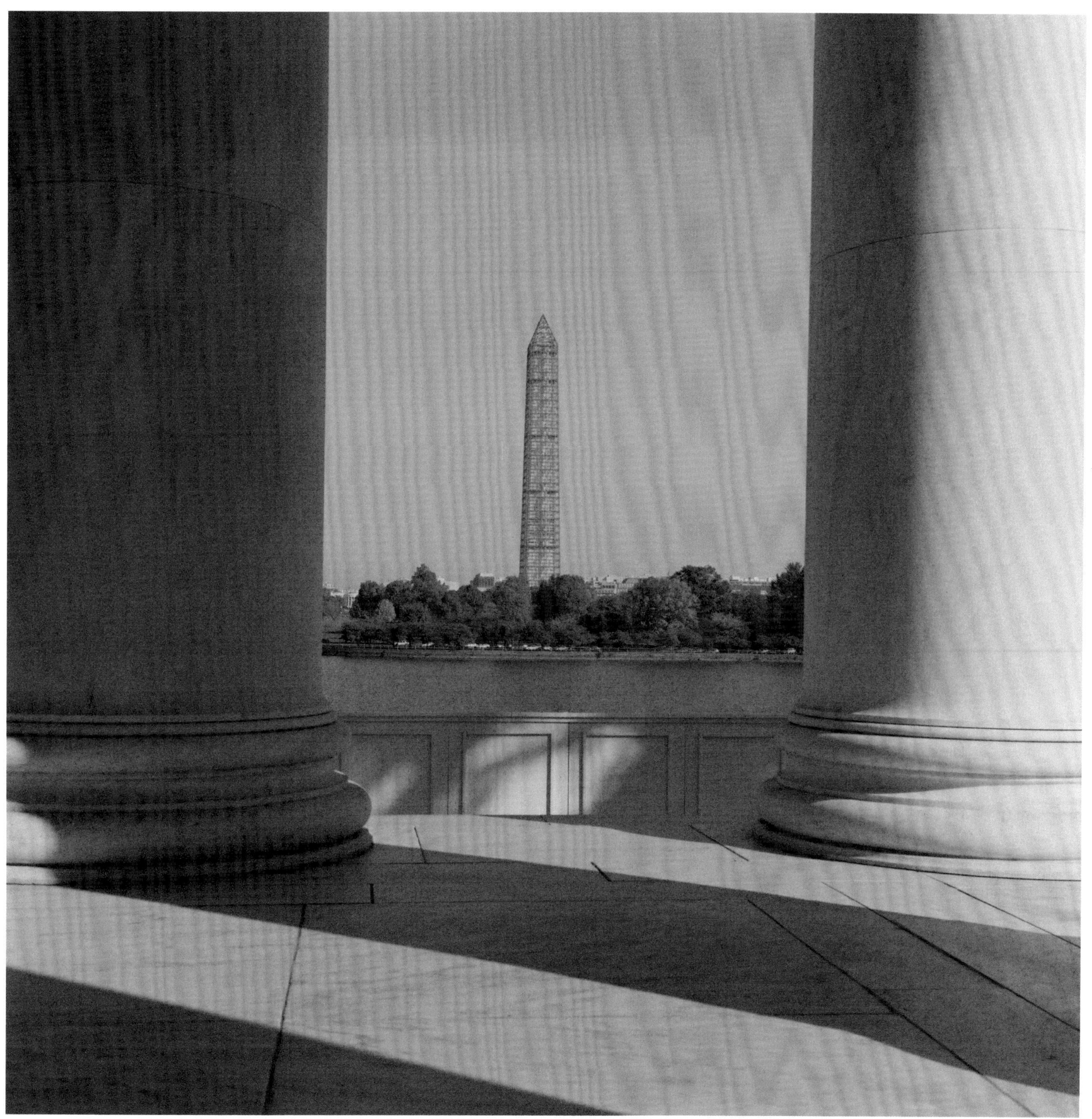

Washington Monument from Jefferson Memorial
Washington, D.C.

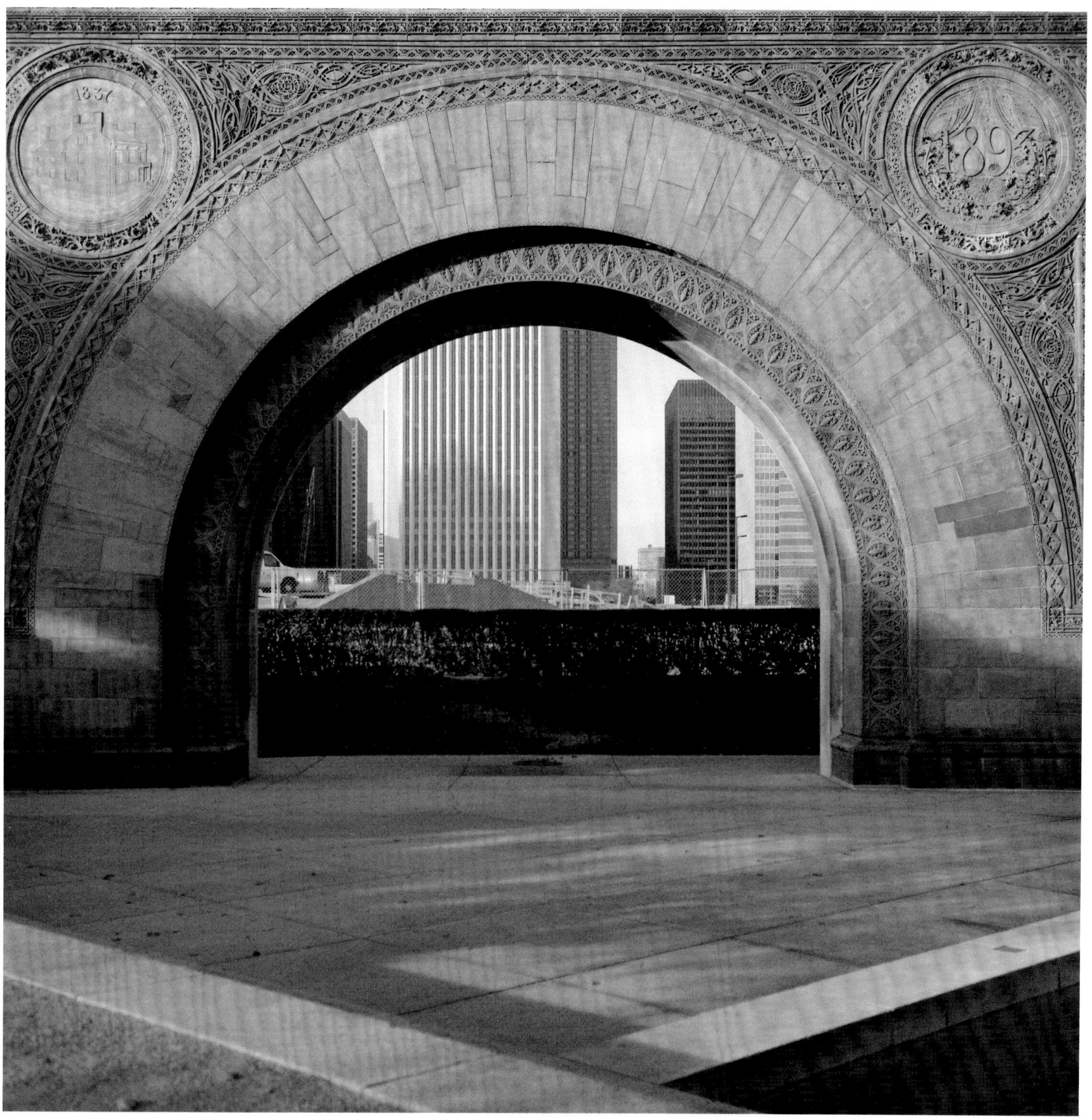

Relocated Chicago Stock Exchange Entry Arch, Art Institute of Chicago
Adler & Sullivan, 1894 • Chicago, Illinois

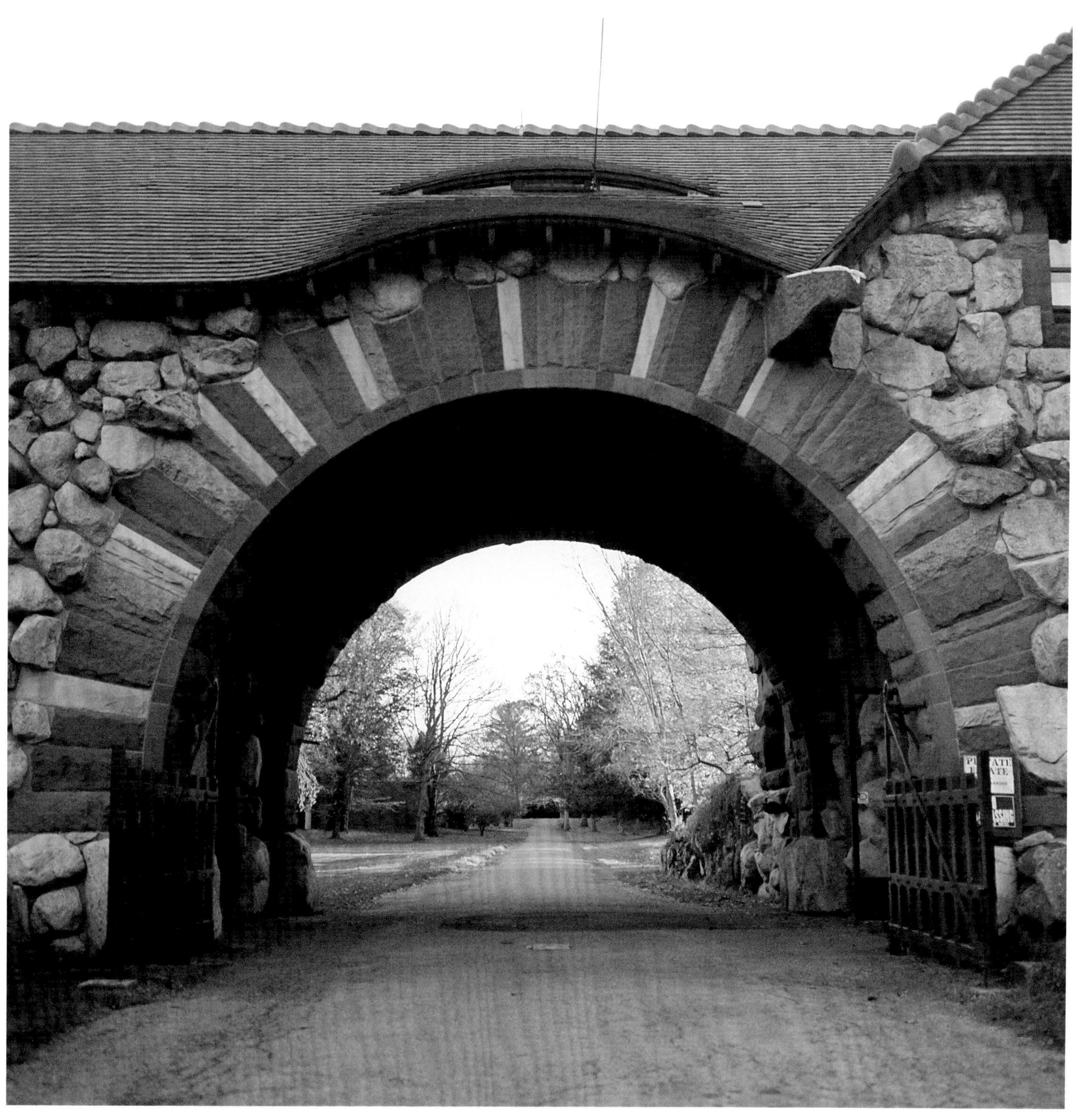

Ames Gate Lodge
H. H. Richardson, 1880–81 • North Easton, Massachusetts

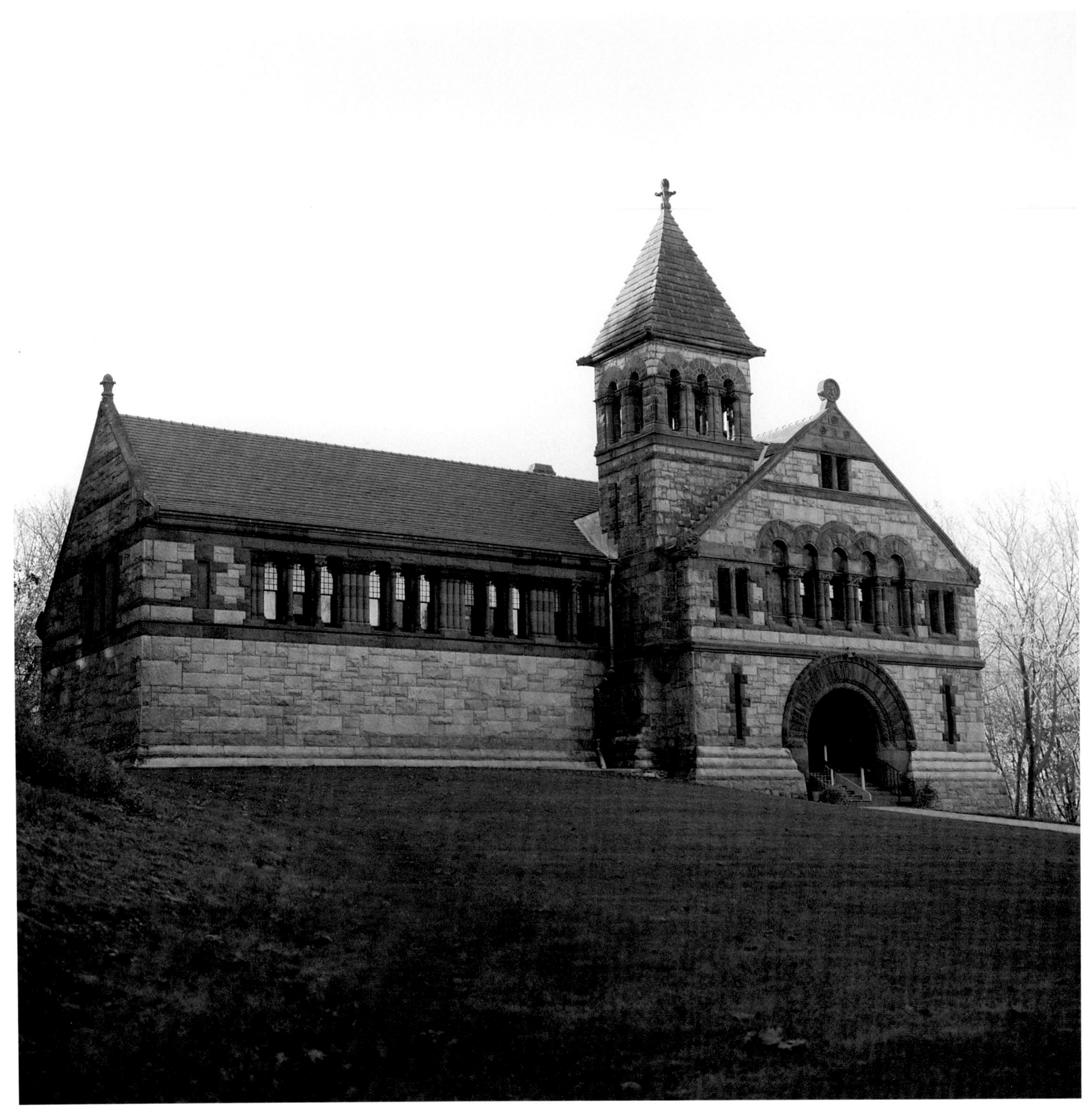

Oliver Ames Free Library
H. H. Richardson, 1877–79 • North Easton, Massachusetts

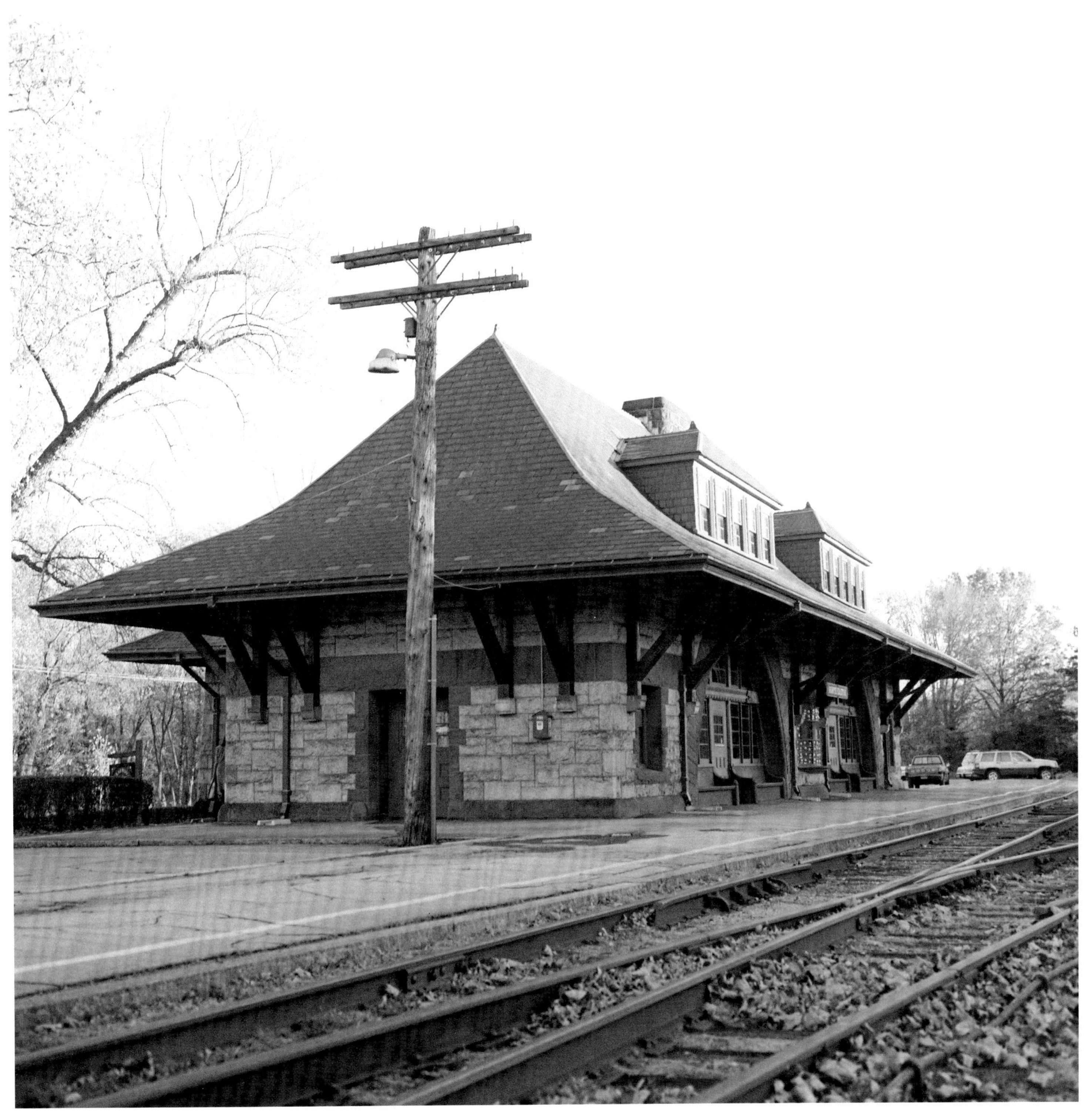

Old Colony Railroad Station
H. H. Richardson, 1881–84 • North Easton, *Massachusetts*

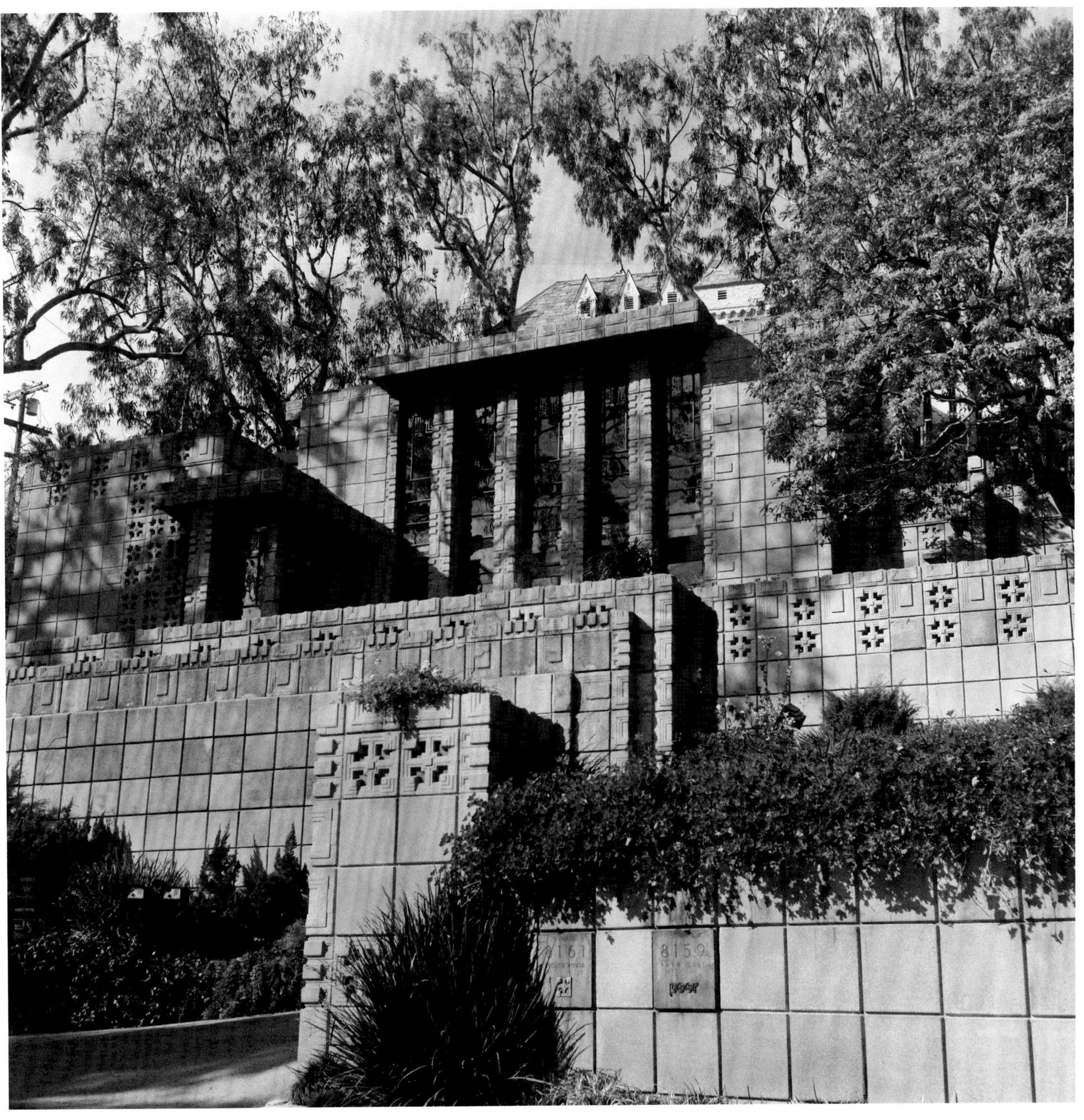

John Storer House
Frank Lloyd Wright, 1923 • Hollywood, California

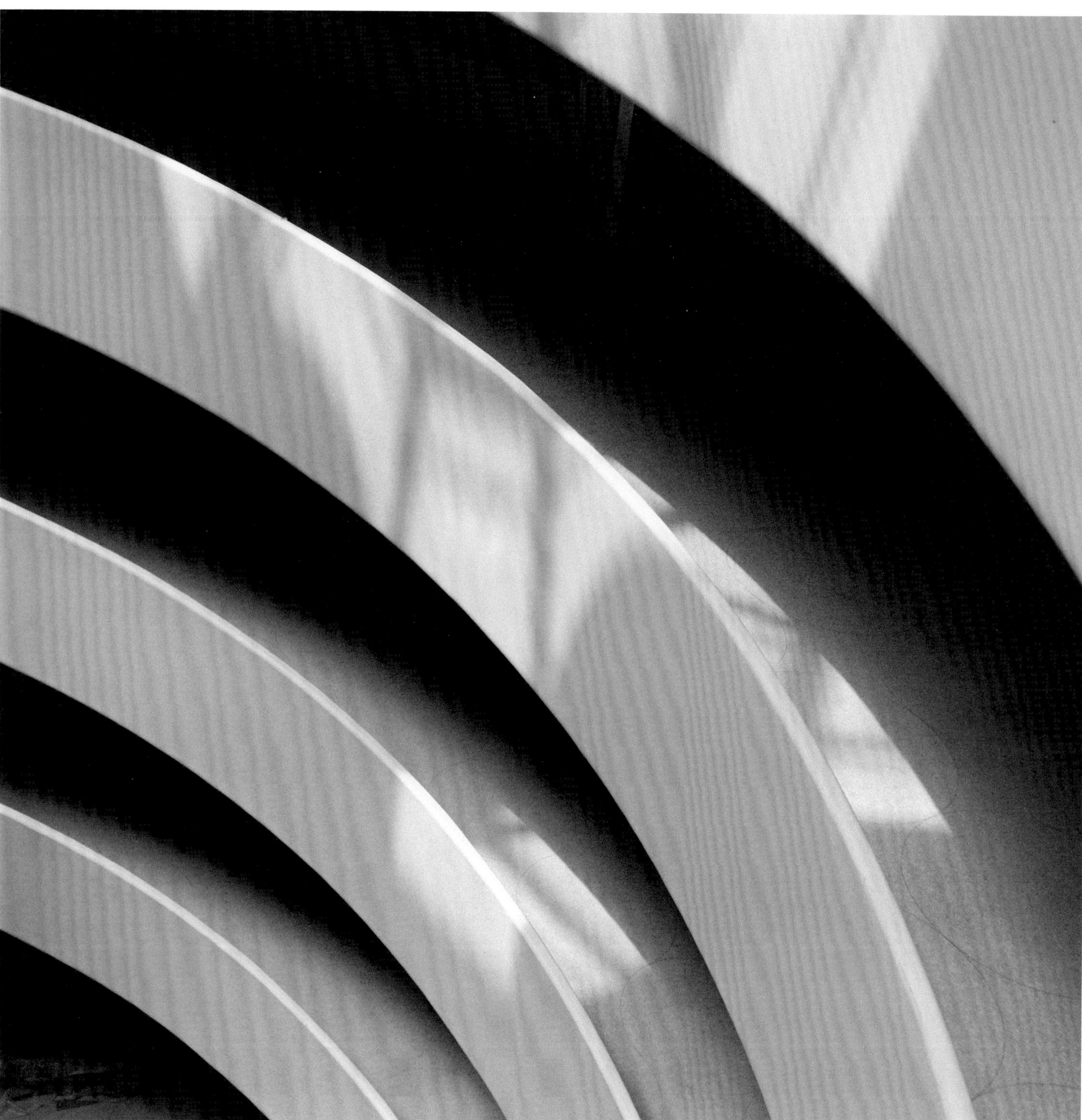

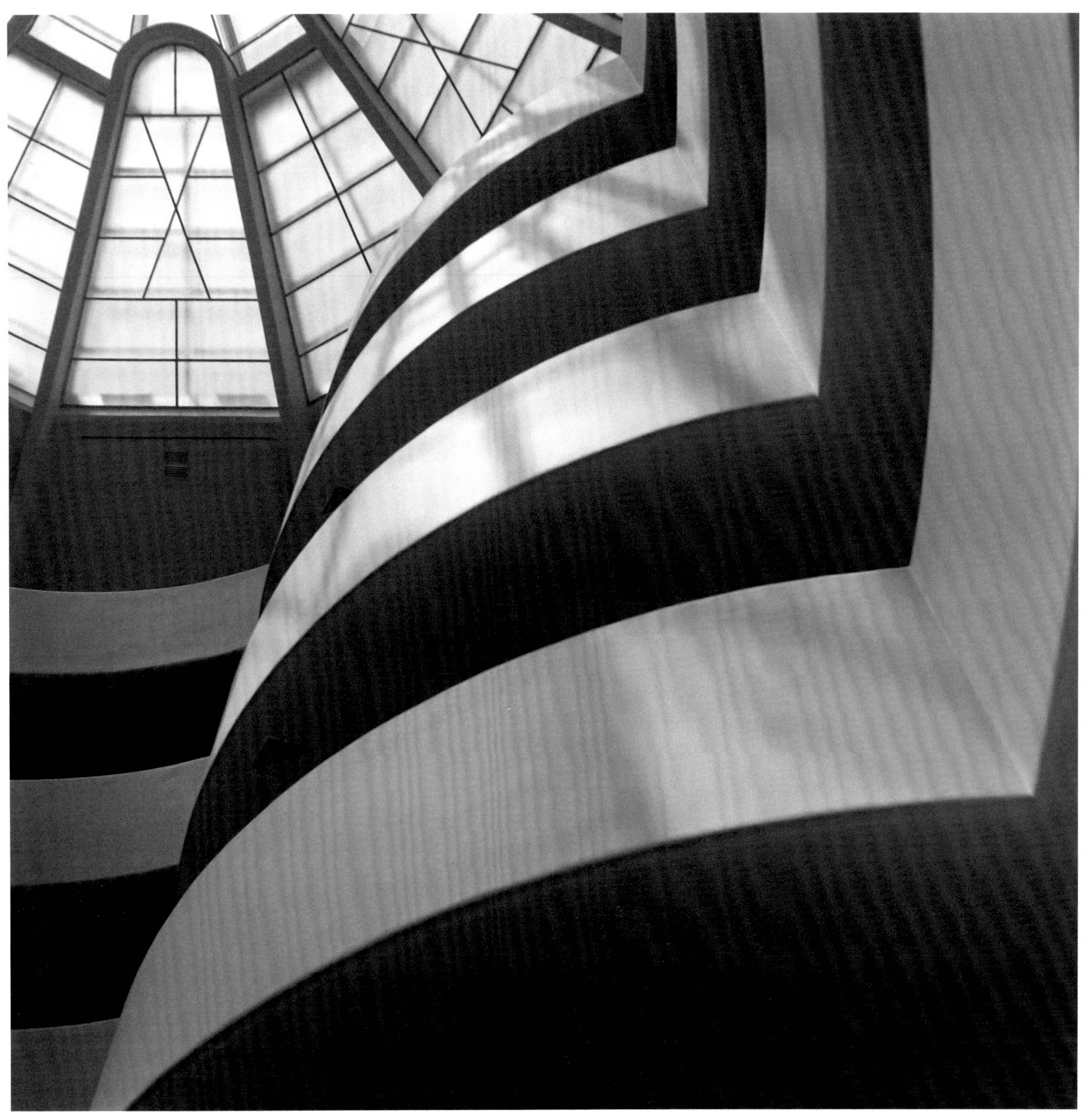

Solomon R. Guggenheim Museum
Frank Lloyd Wright, 1956–59 • *New York, New York*

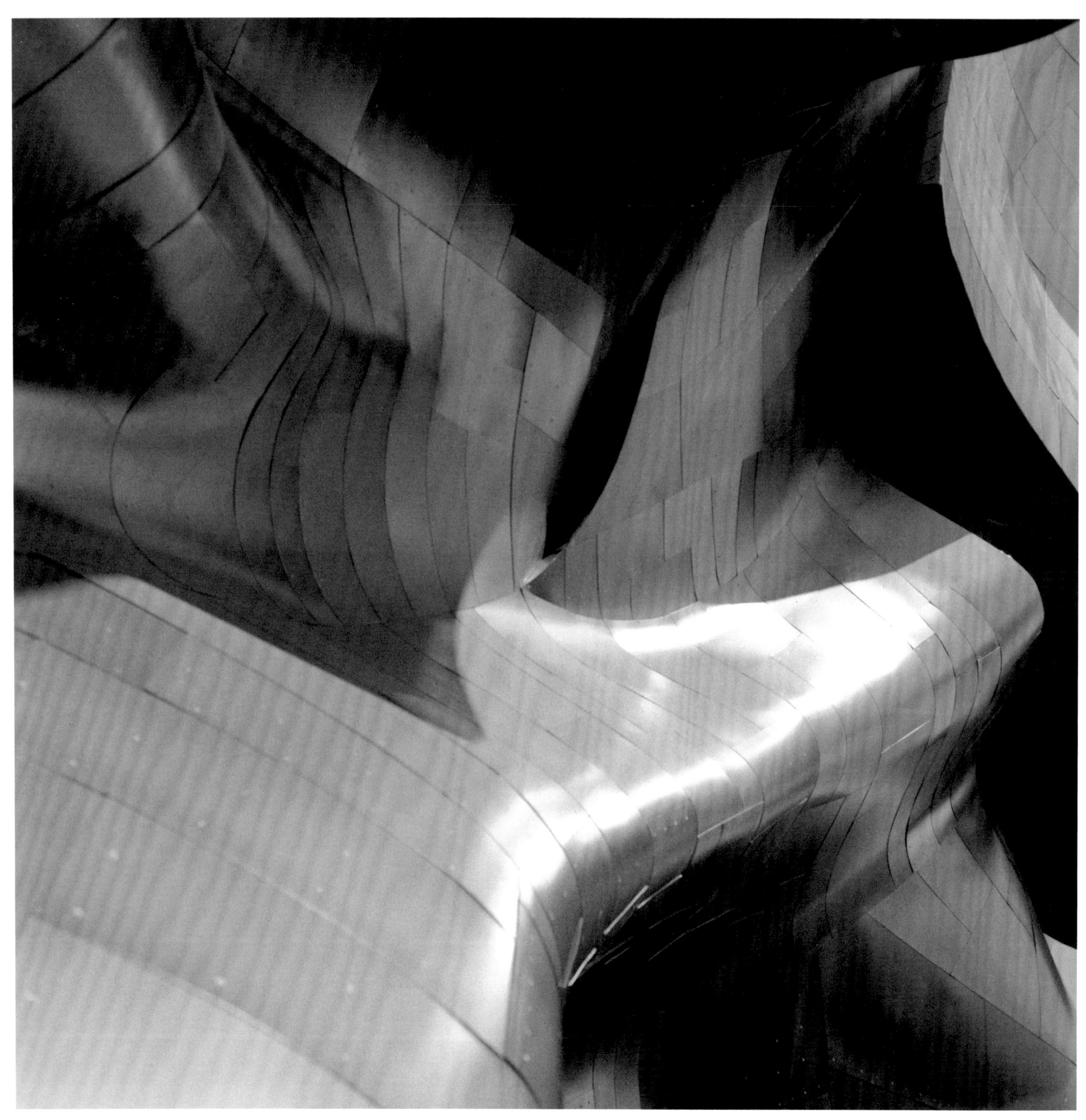

Experience Music Project
Frank O. Gehry, 1996–2000 • Seattle, Washington

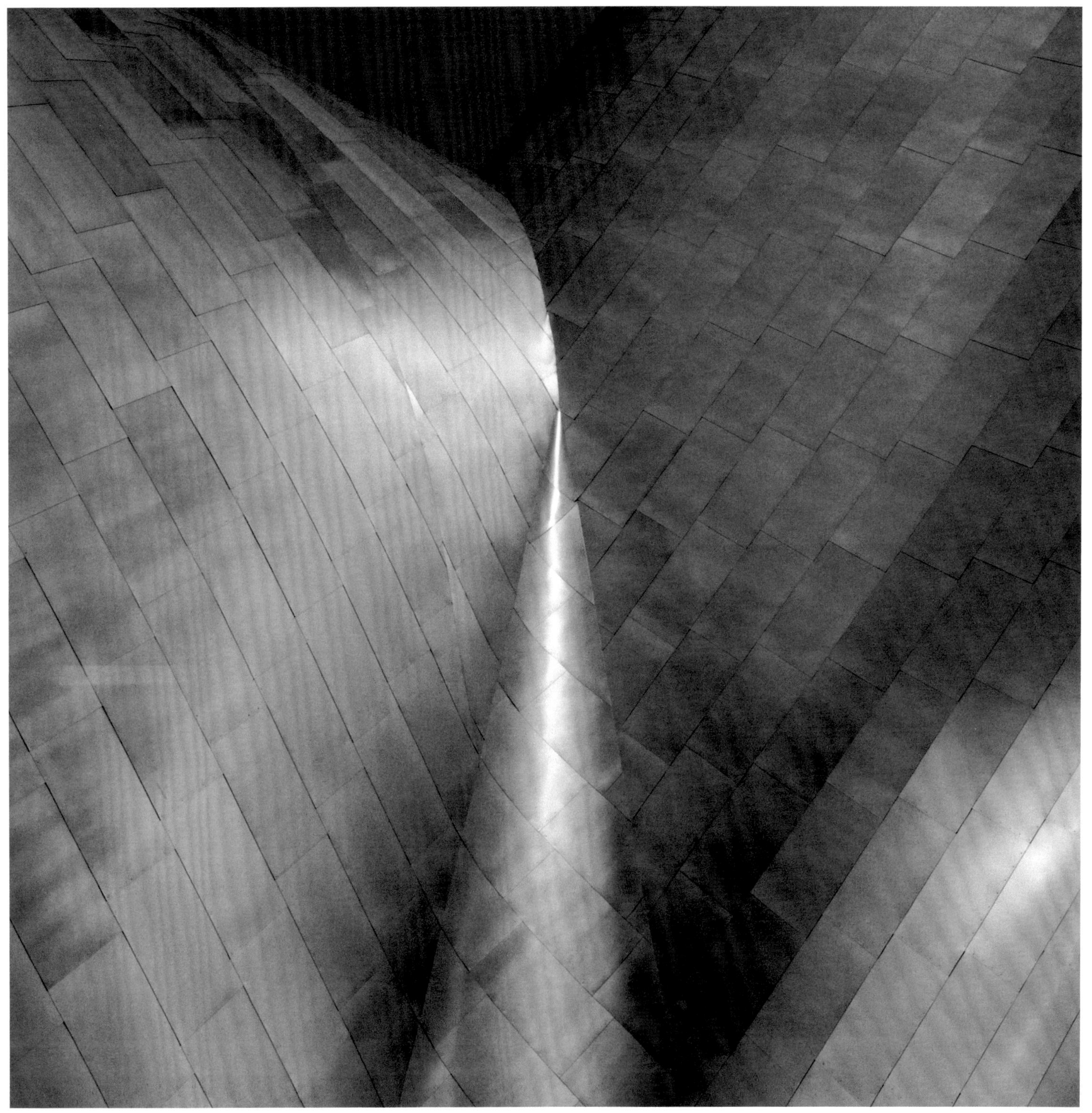

Richard B. Fisher Center for the Performing Arts at Bard College
Frank O. Gehry, 2003 • Annandale-on-Hudson, New York

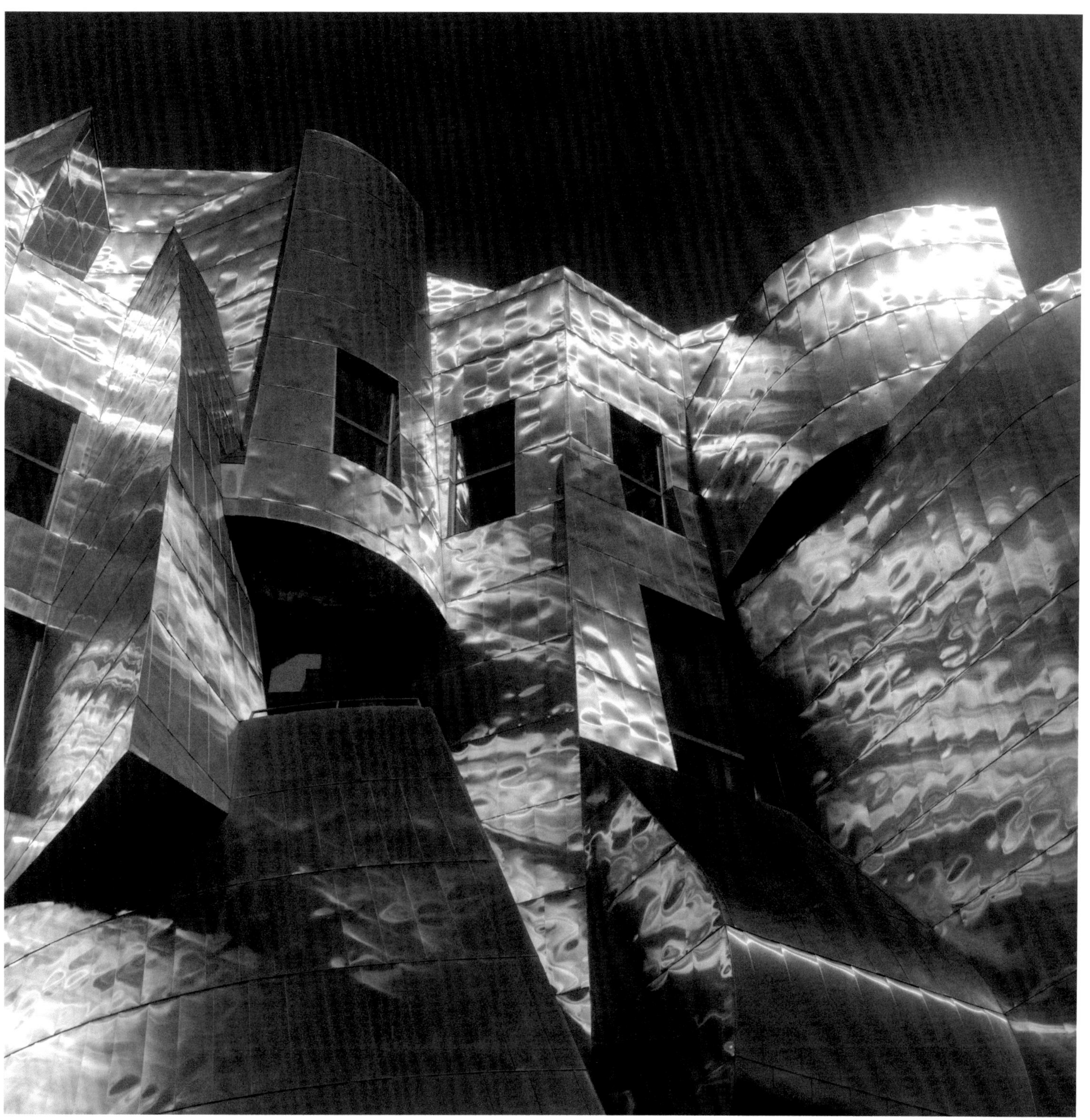

Weisman Art Museum, University of Minnesota
Frank O. Gehry, 1993 • Minneapolis, Minnesota

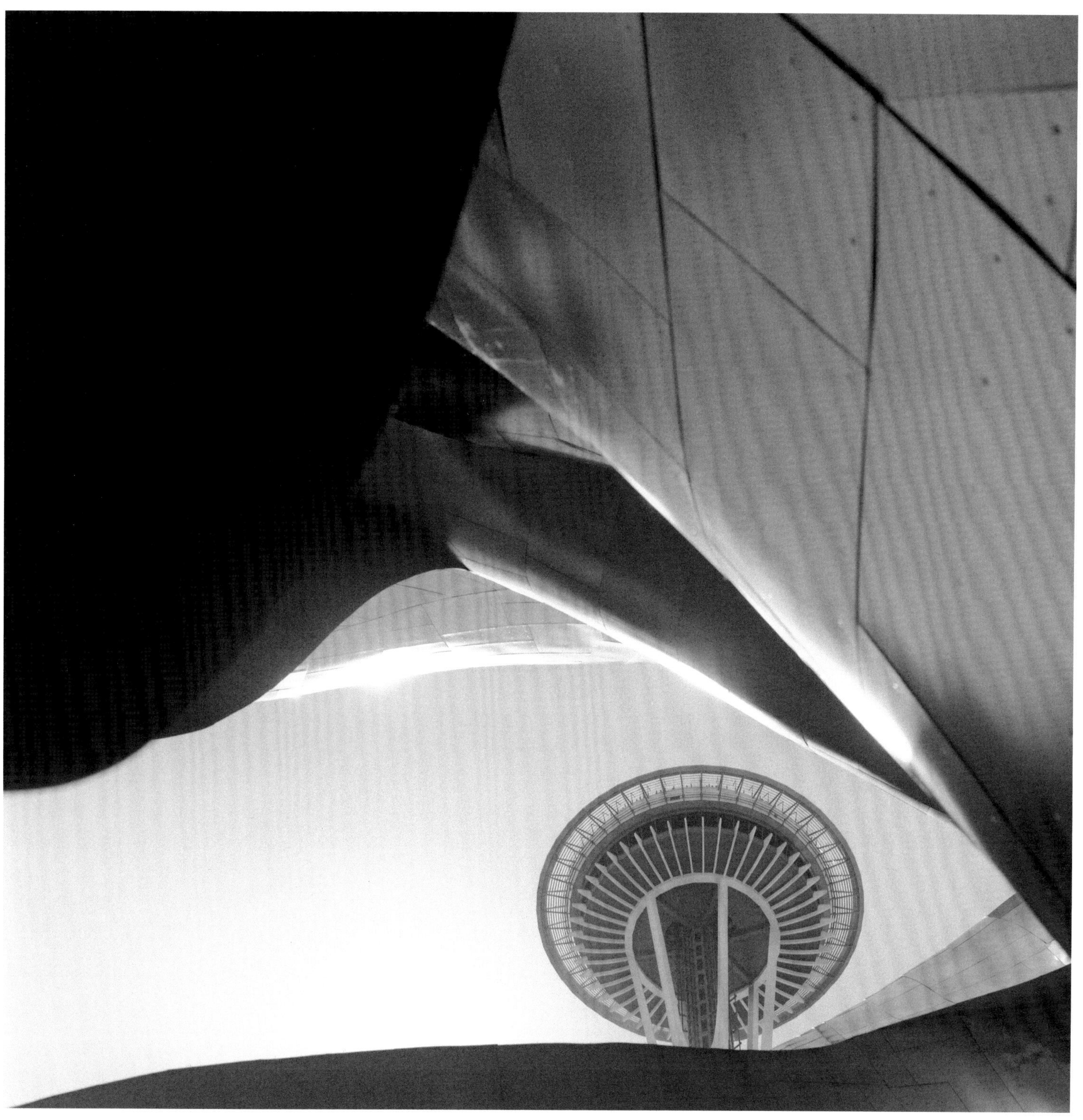

Experience Music Project and Space Needle
Seattle, Washington

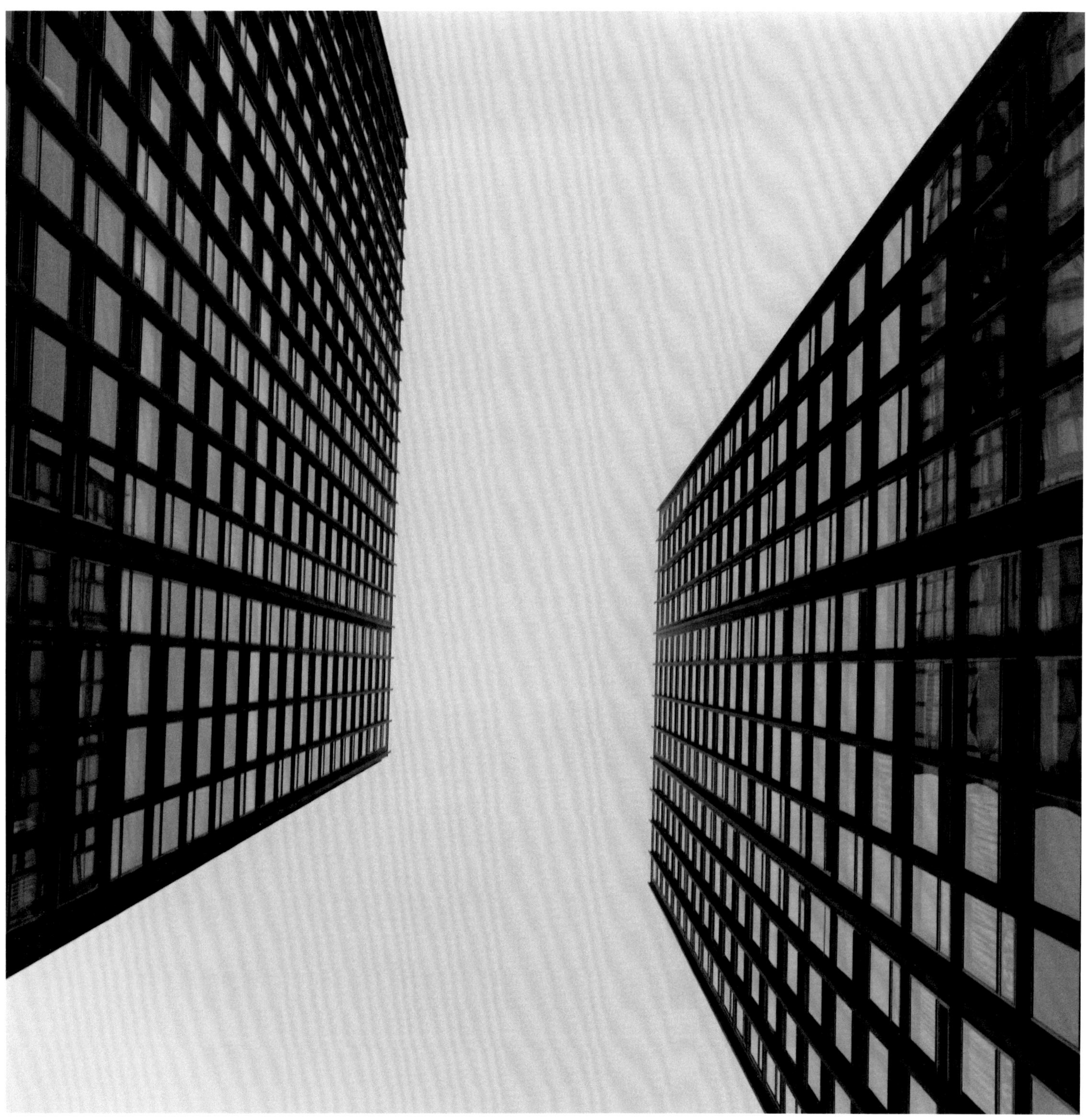

860–880 Lake Shore Drive
Ludwig Mies van der Rohe, 1951 • Chicago, Illinois

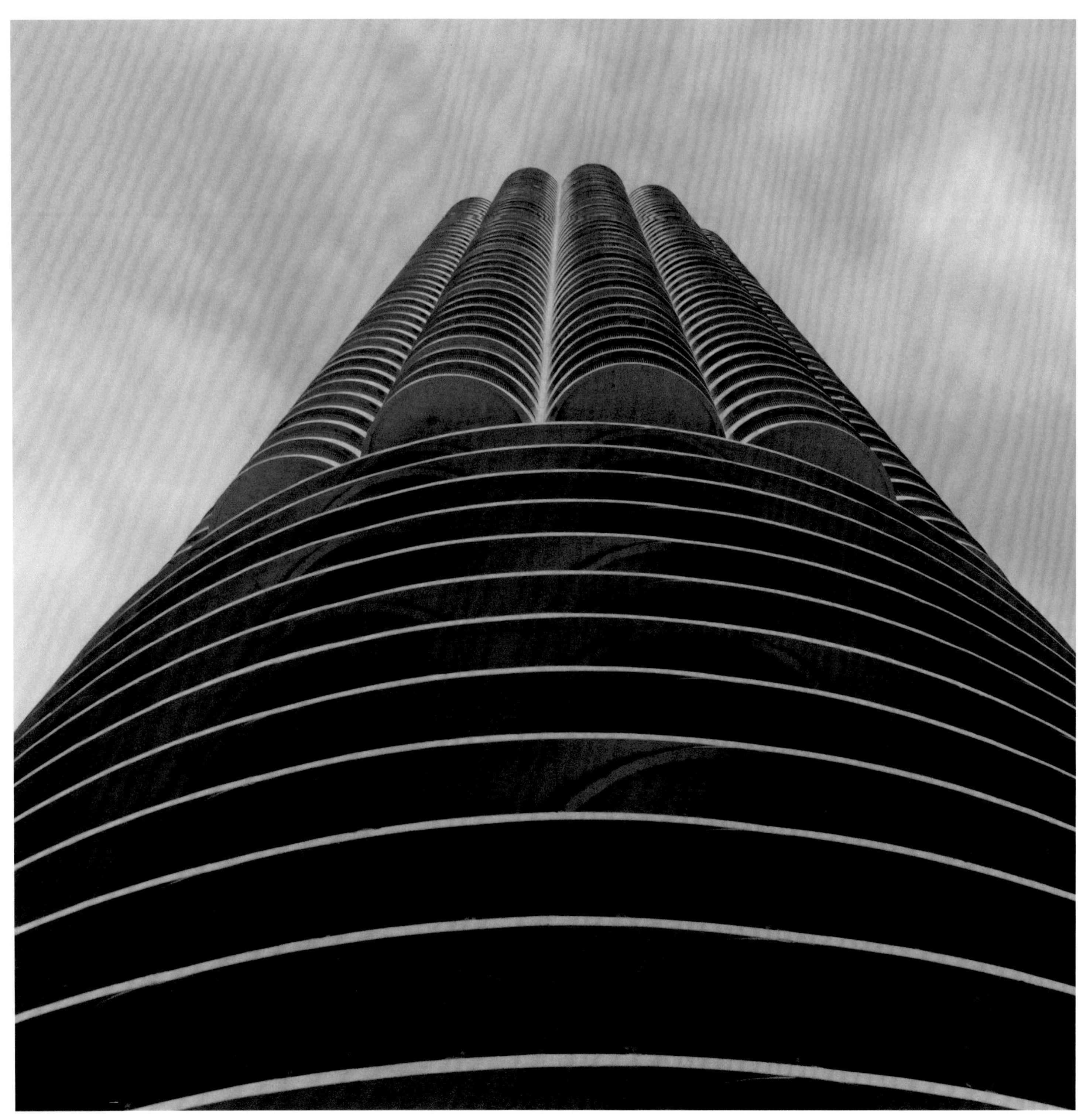

Marina City
Bertrand Goldberg Associates, 1964 • Chicago, Illinois

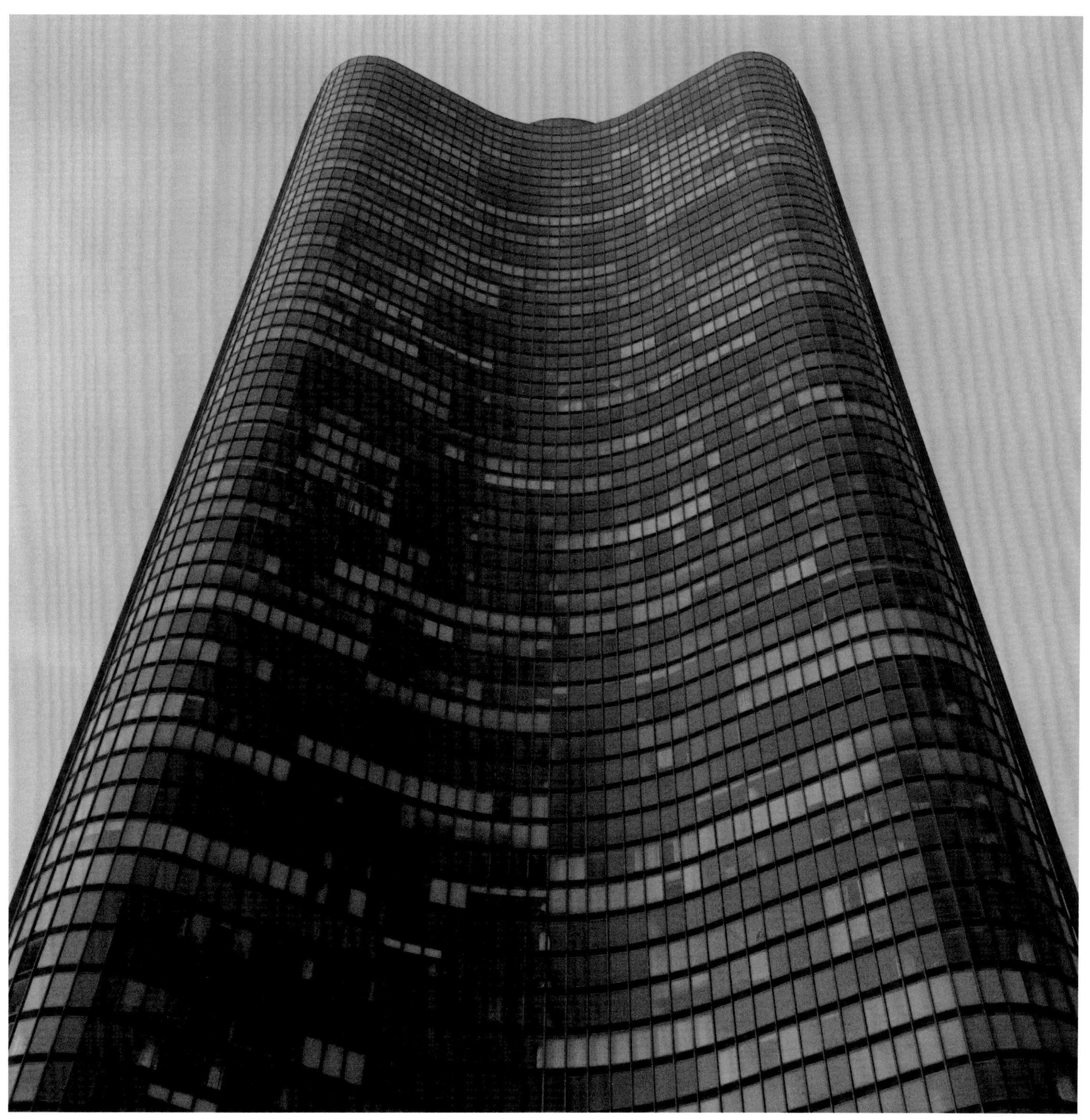

Lake Point Tower
Schipporeit-Heinrich Associates, 1968 • Chicago, Illinois

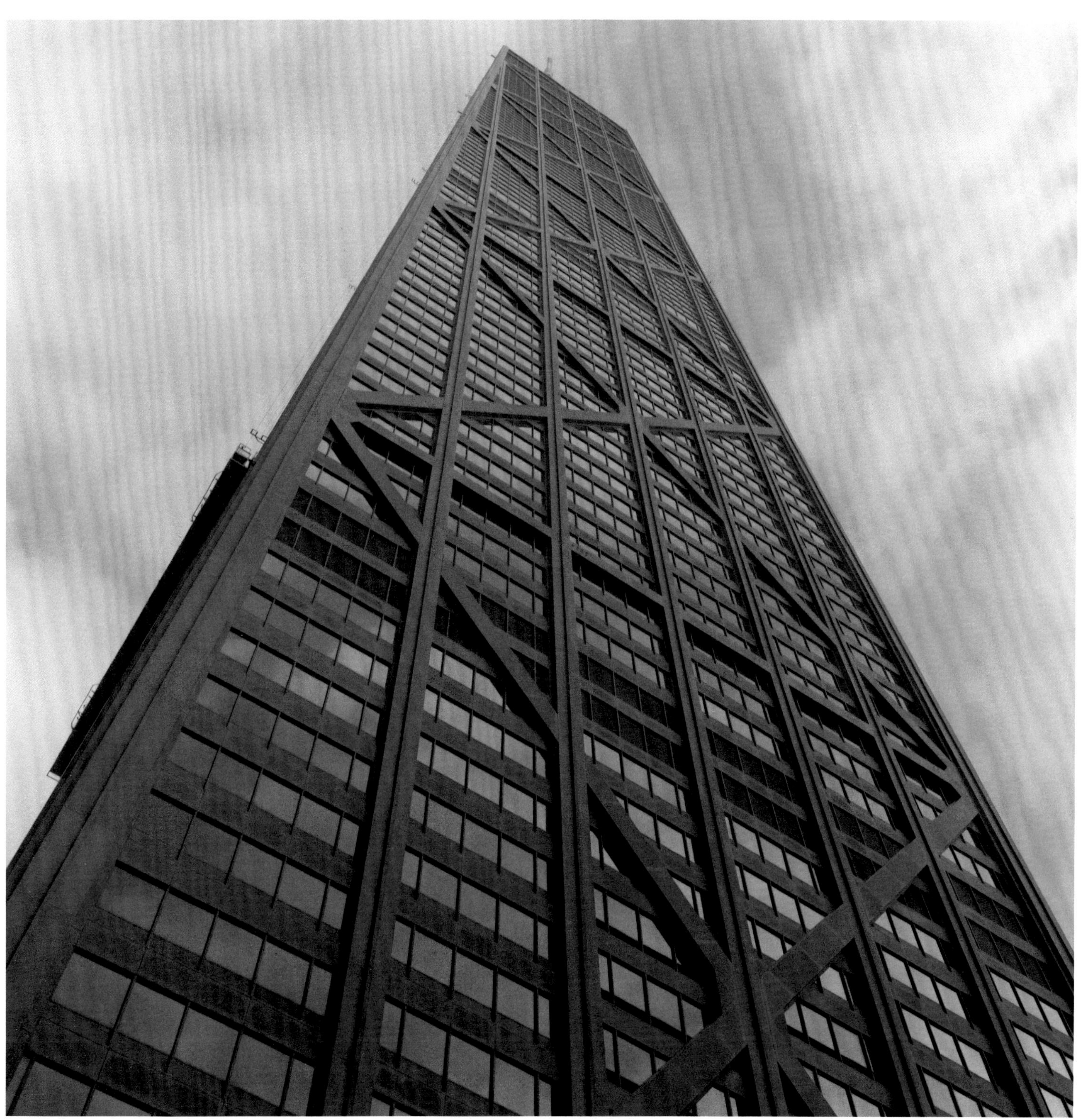

John Hancock Center
Skidmore, Owings & Merrill, 1970 • Chicago, Illinois

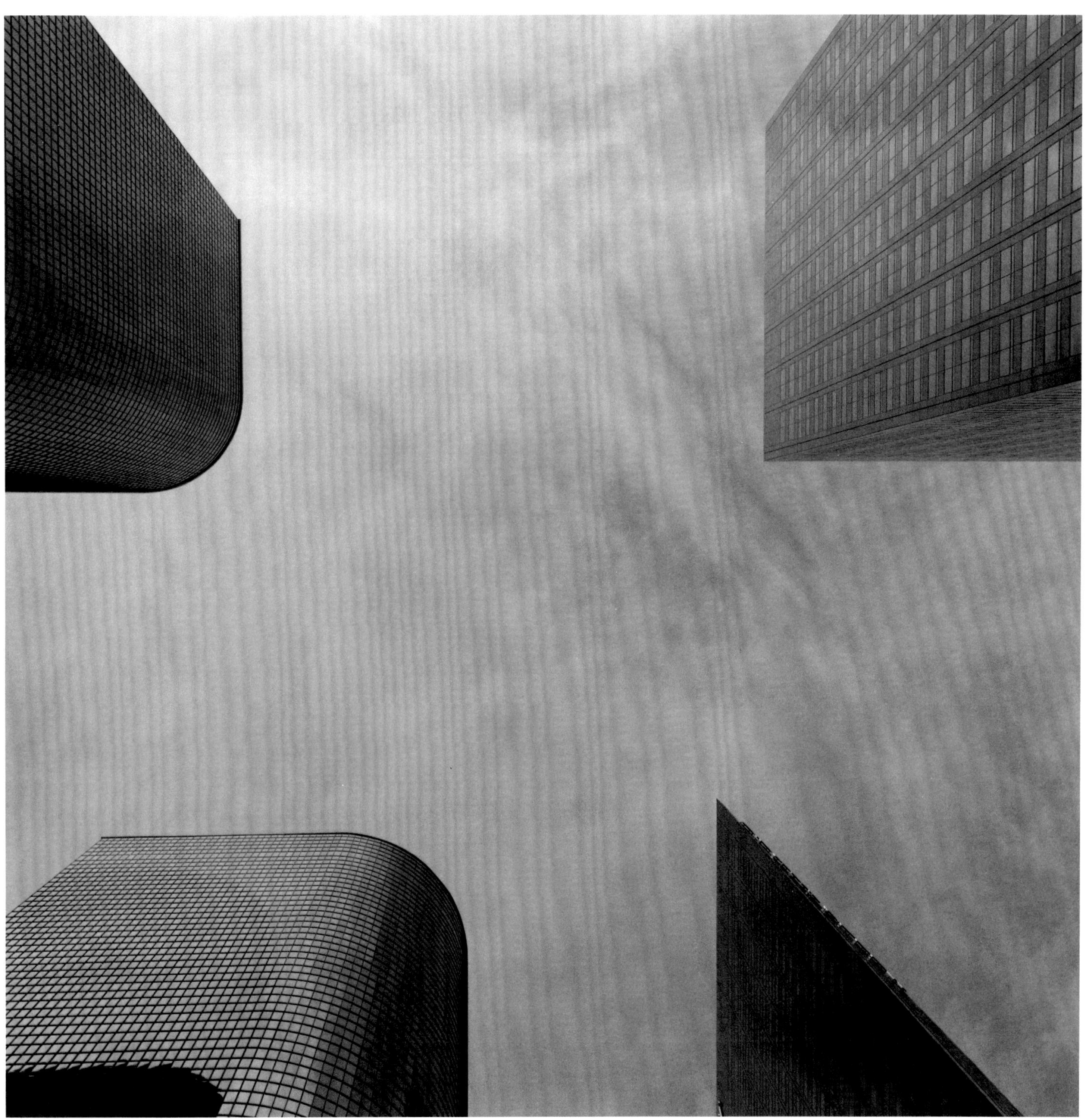

Downtown Los Angeles, California

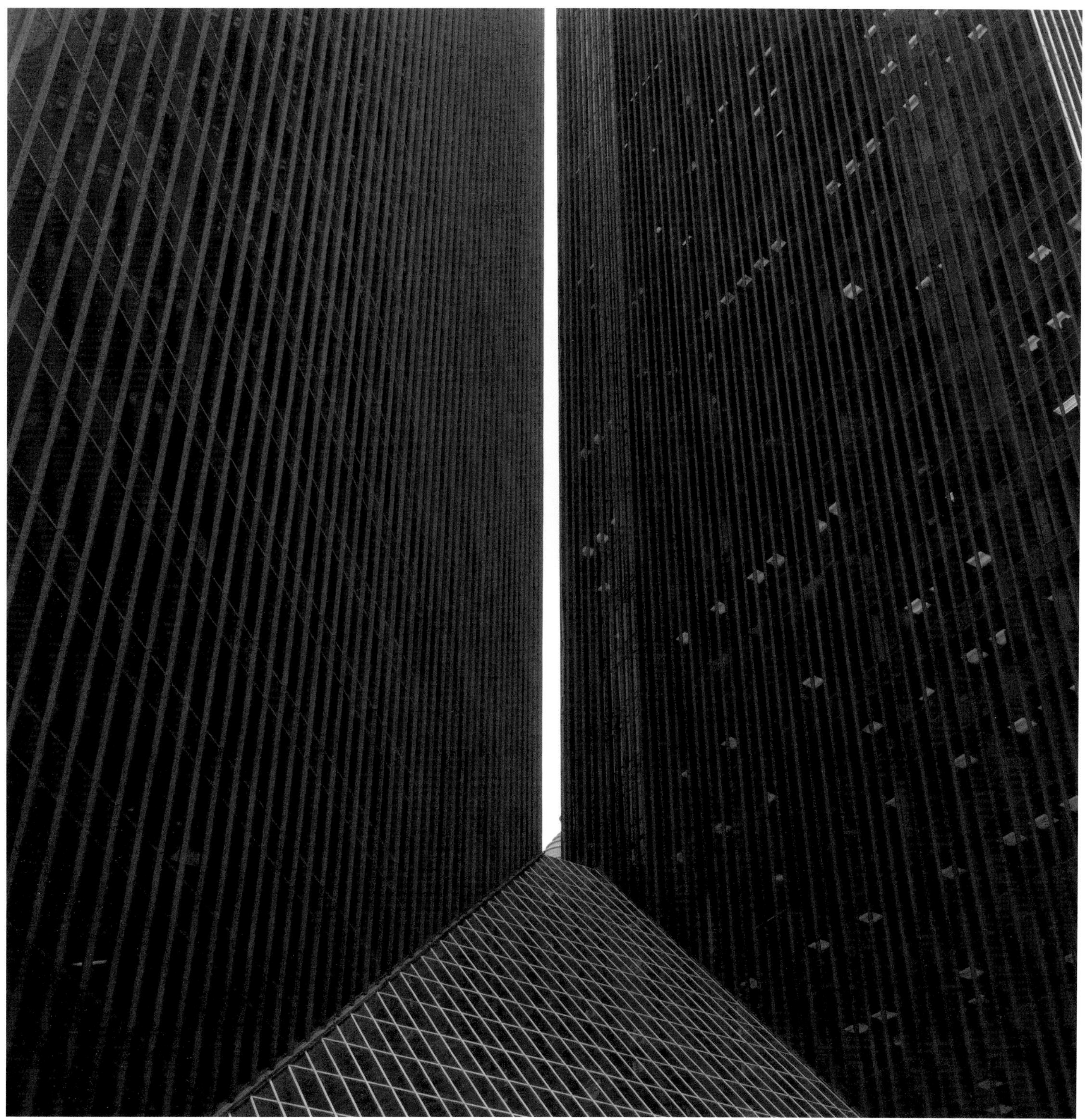

Pennzoil Place
Johnson/Burgee Architects, 1976 • Houston, Texas

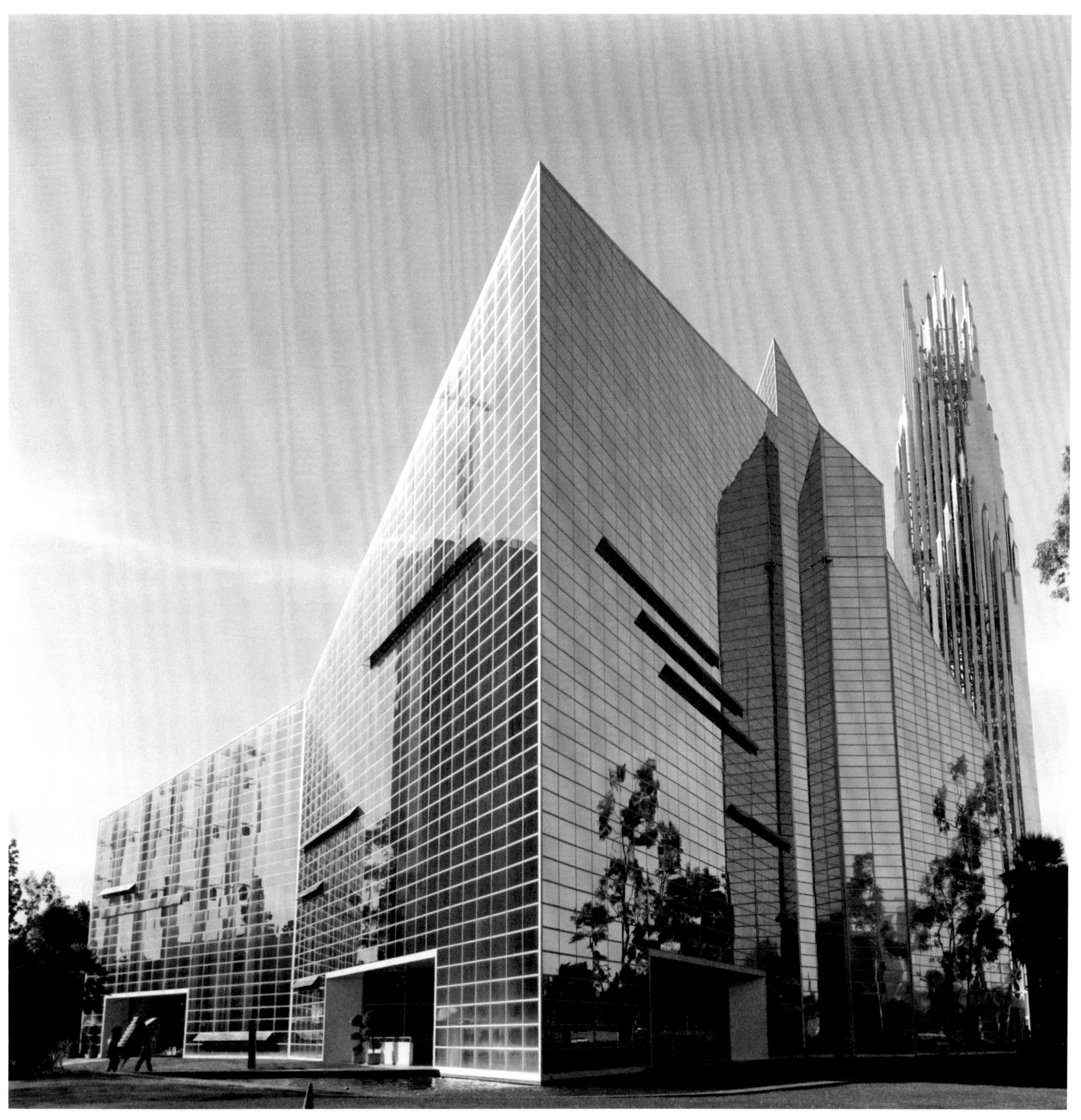

Crystal Cathedral, Garden Grove Community Church
Johnson/Burgee Architects, 1980 • Garden Grove, California

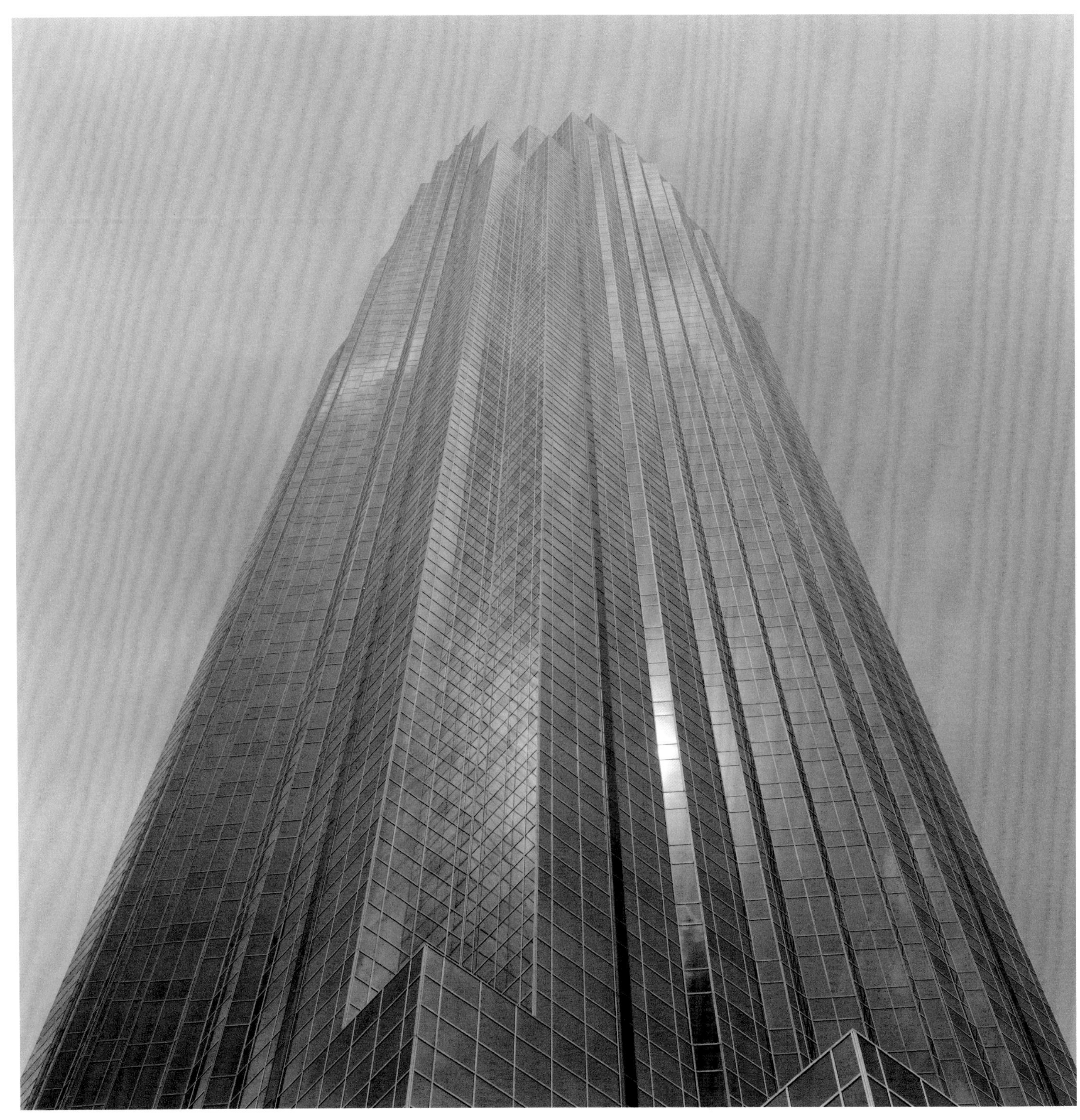

Transco Tower
Philip Johnson, 1984 • Houston, Texas

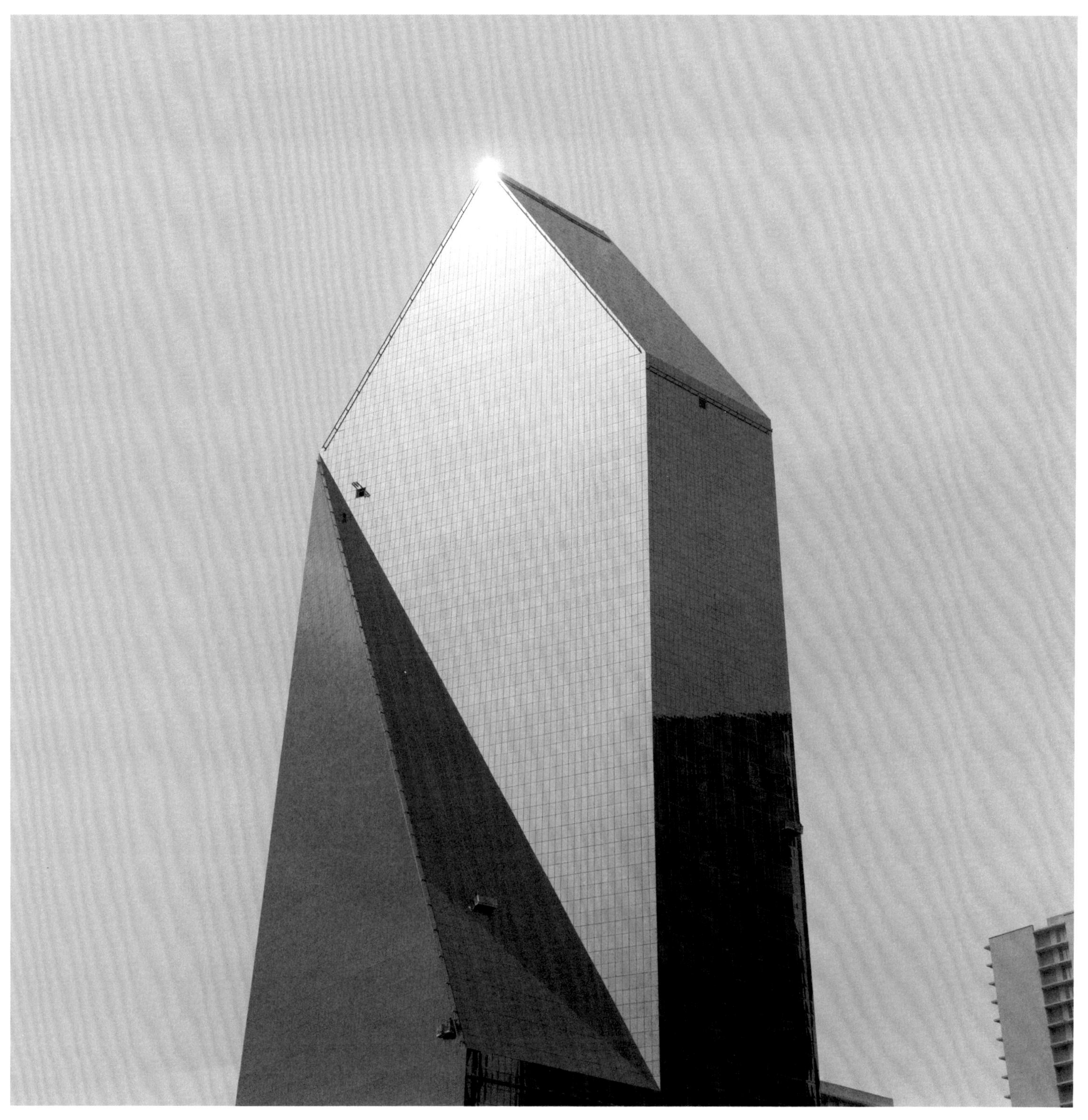

Fountain Place
I. M. Pei & Partners, 1986 • Dallas, Texas

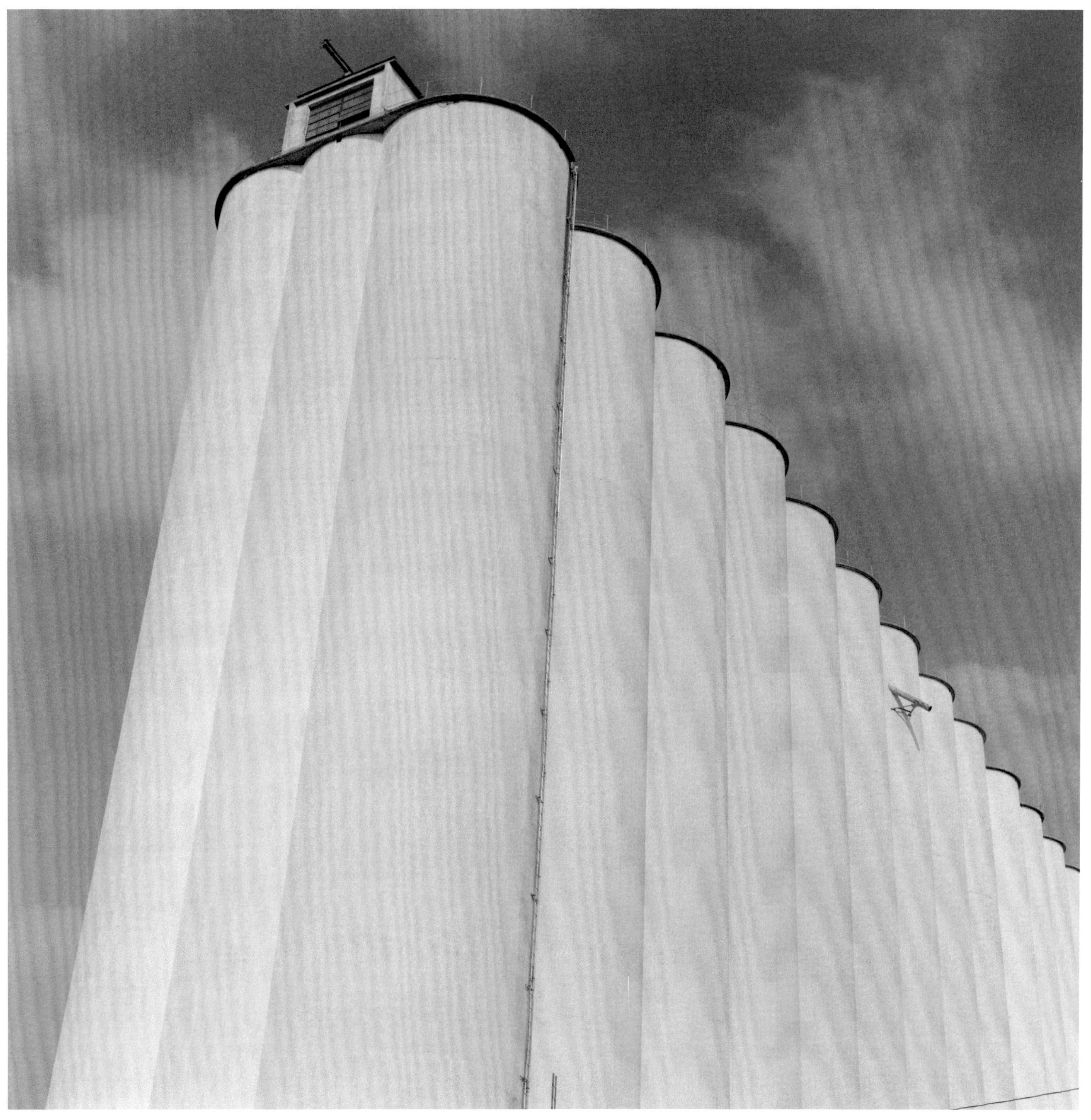

Grain Elevator
Amarillo, Texas

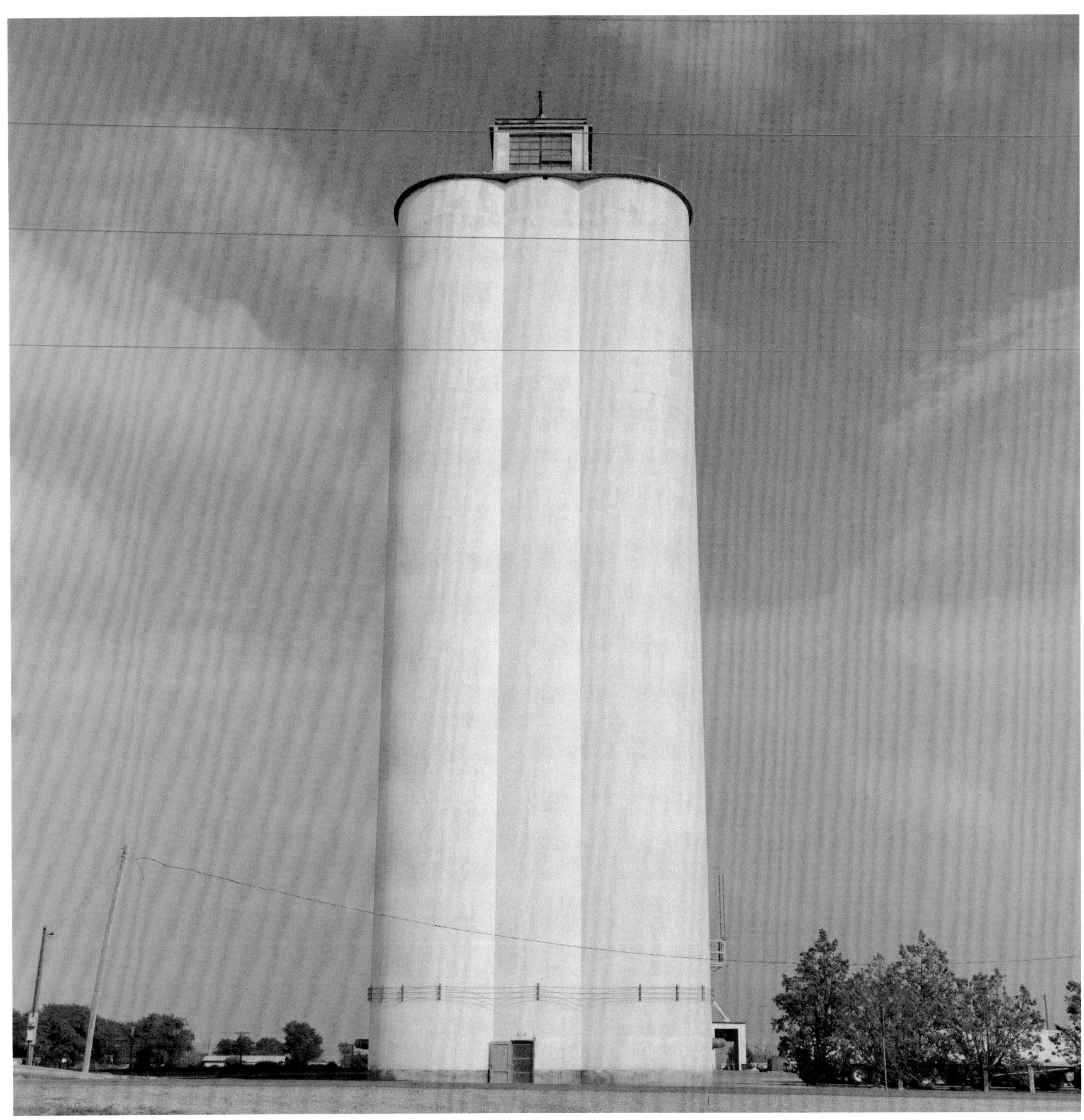

Grain Elevator
Amarillo, Texas

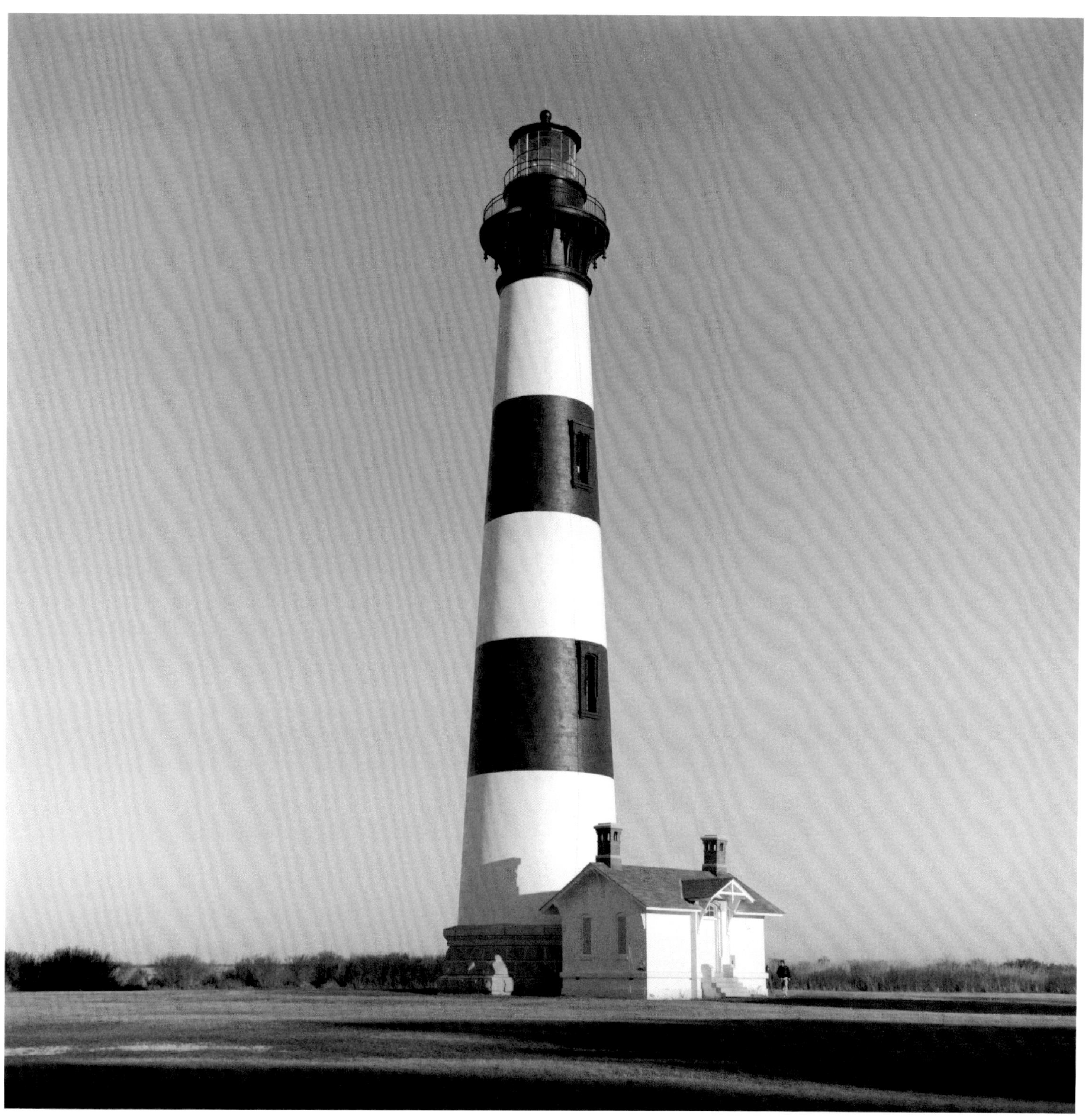

Bodie Lighthouse
1872 • Bodie Island, North Carolina

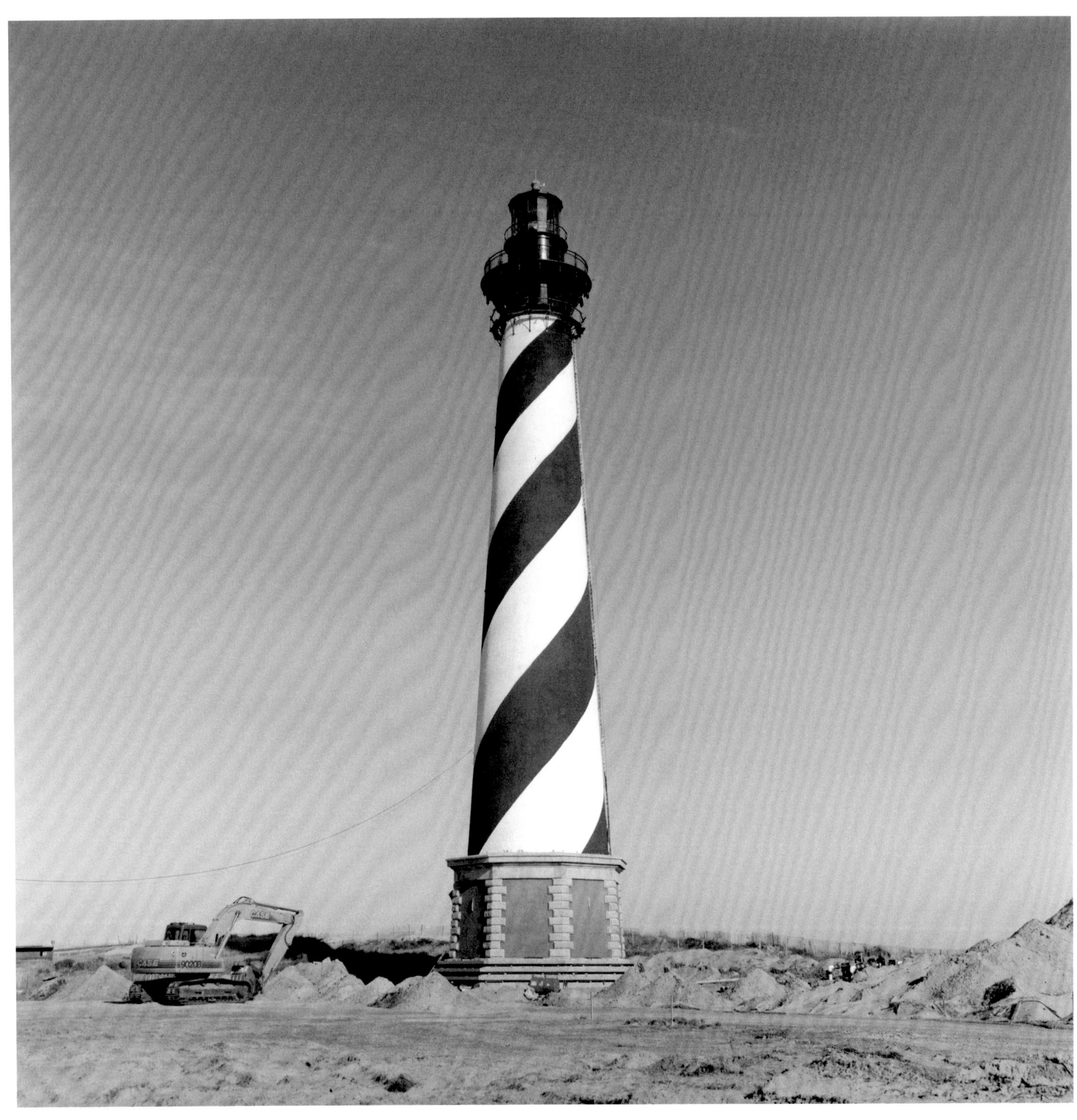

Cape Hatteras Lighthouse
1869 • *Hatteras Island, North Carolina*

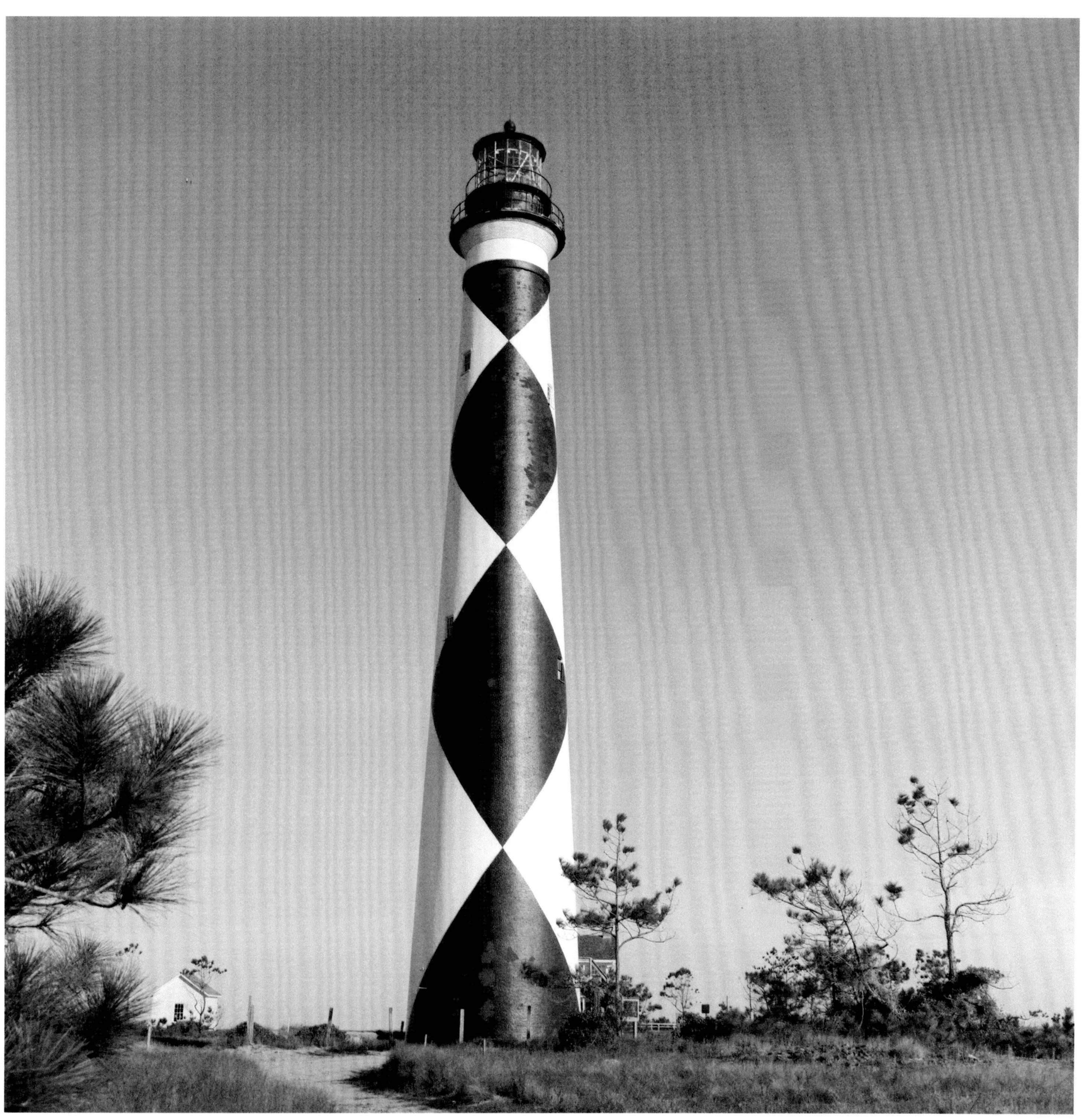

Cape Lookout Lighthouse
1859 • *Core Banks, North Carolina*

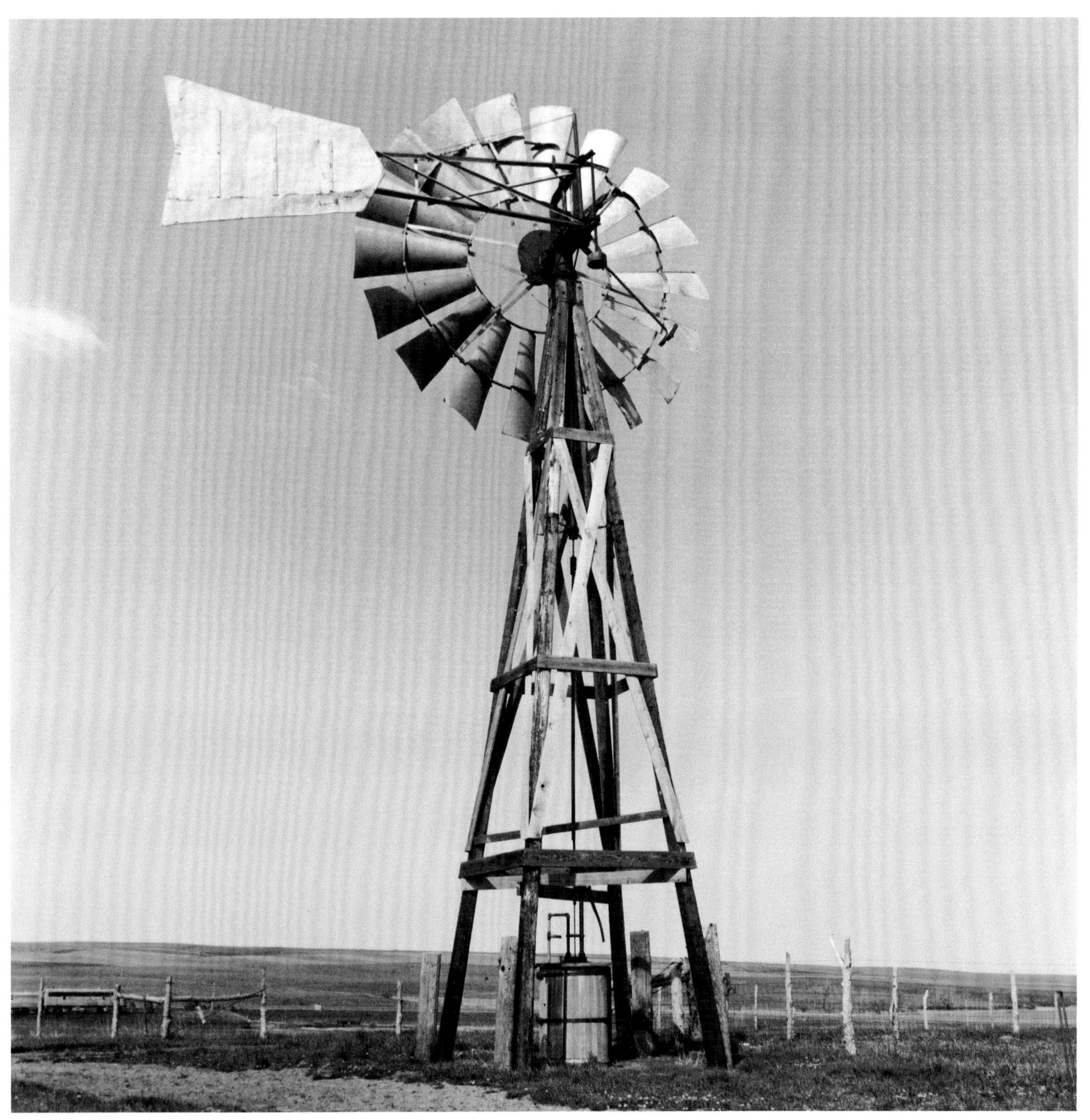

Windmill
Great Plains, South Dakota

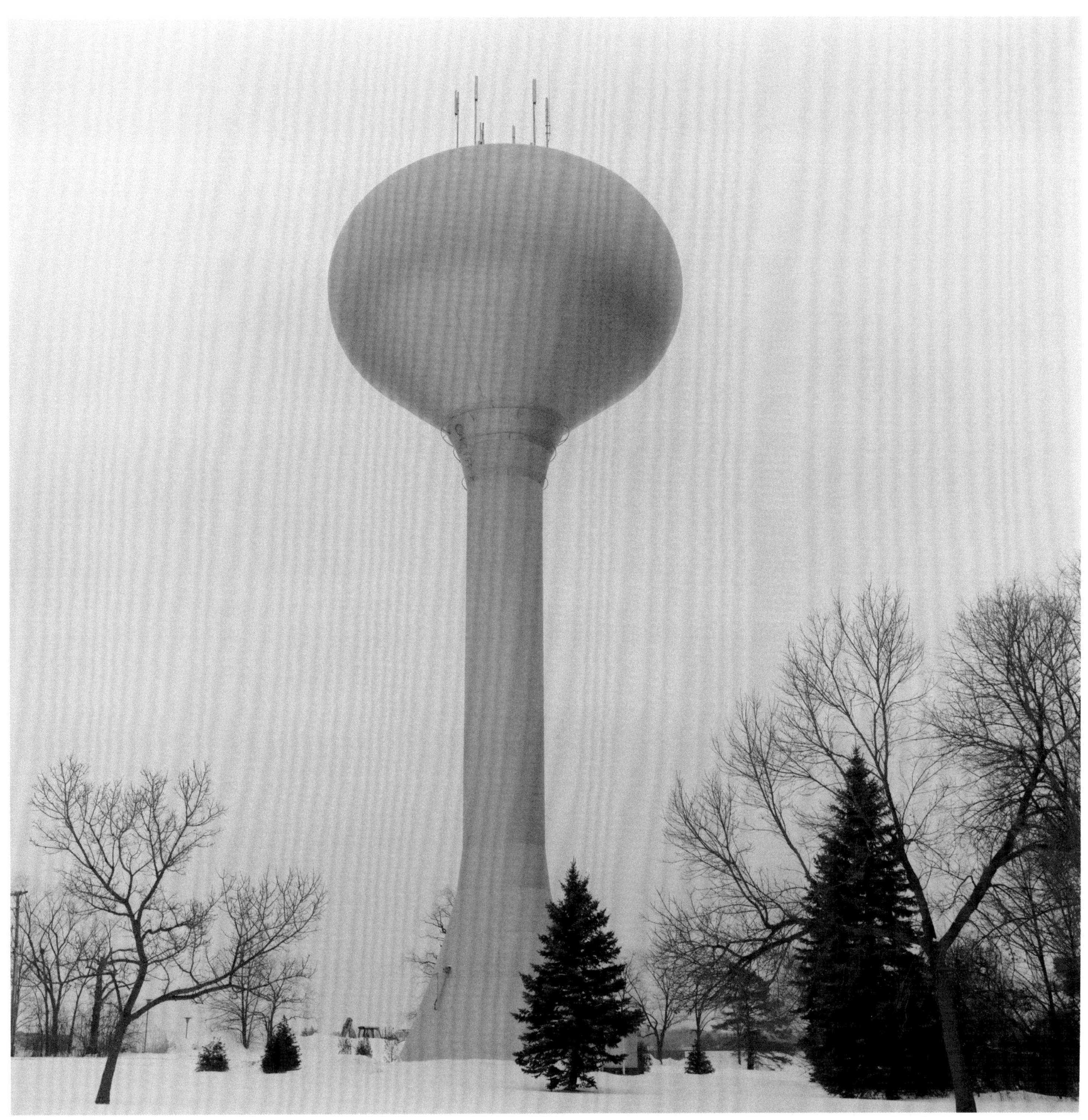

Water Tower
Ypsilanti, Michigan

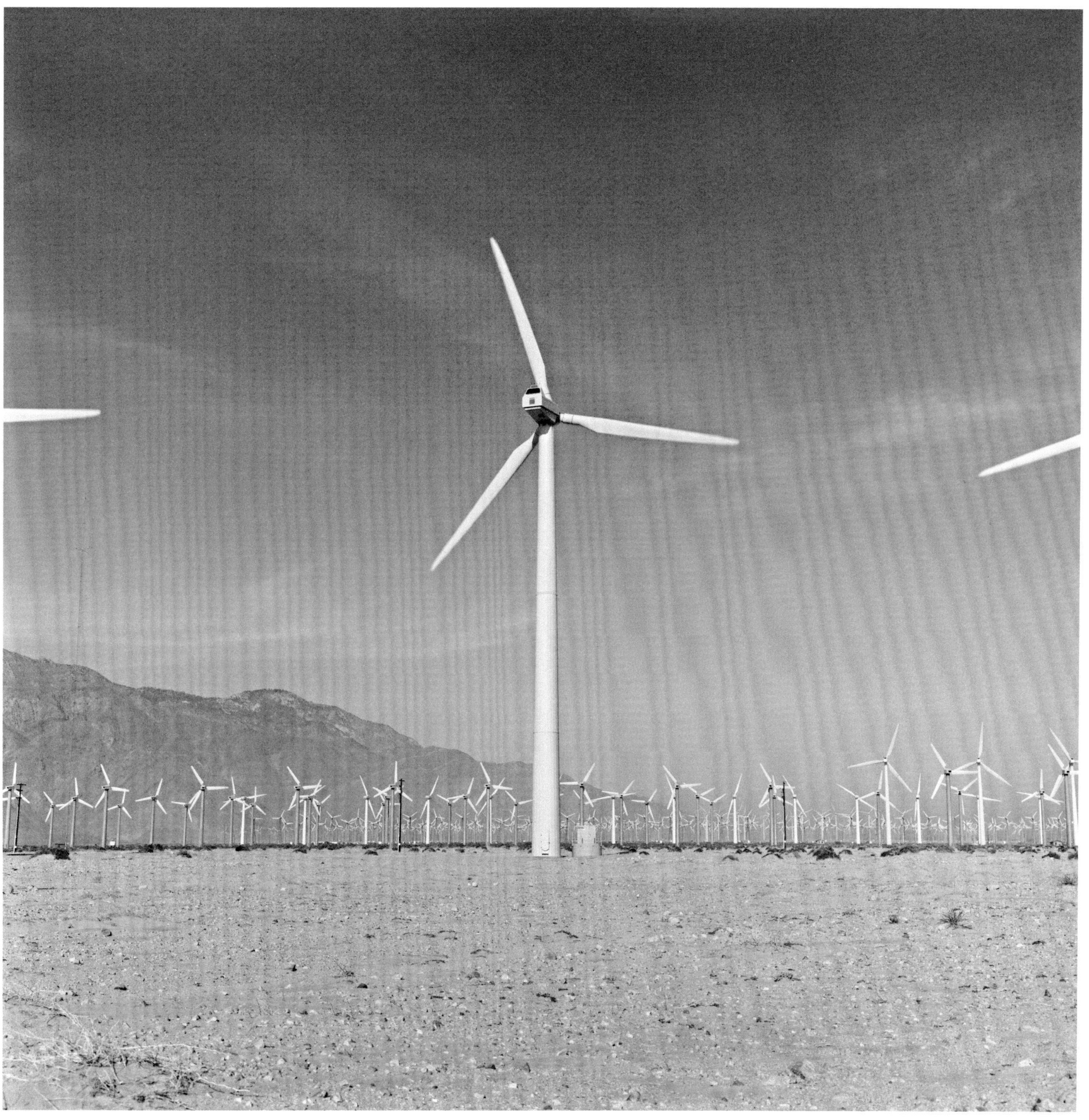

Wind Turbines
Palm Springs, California

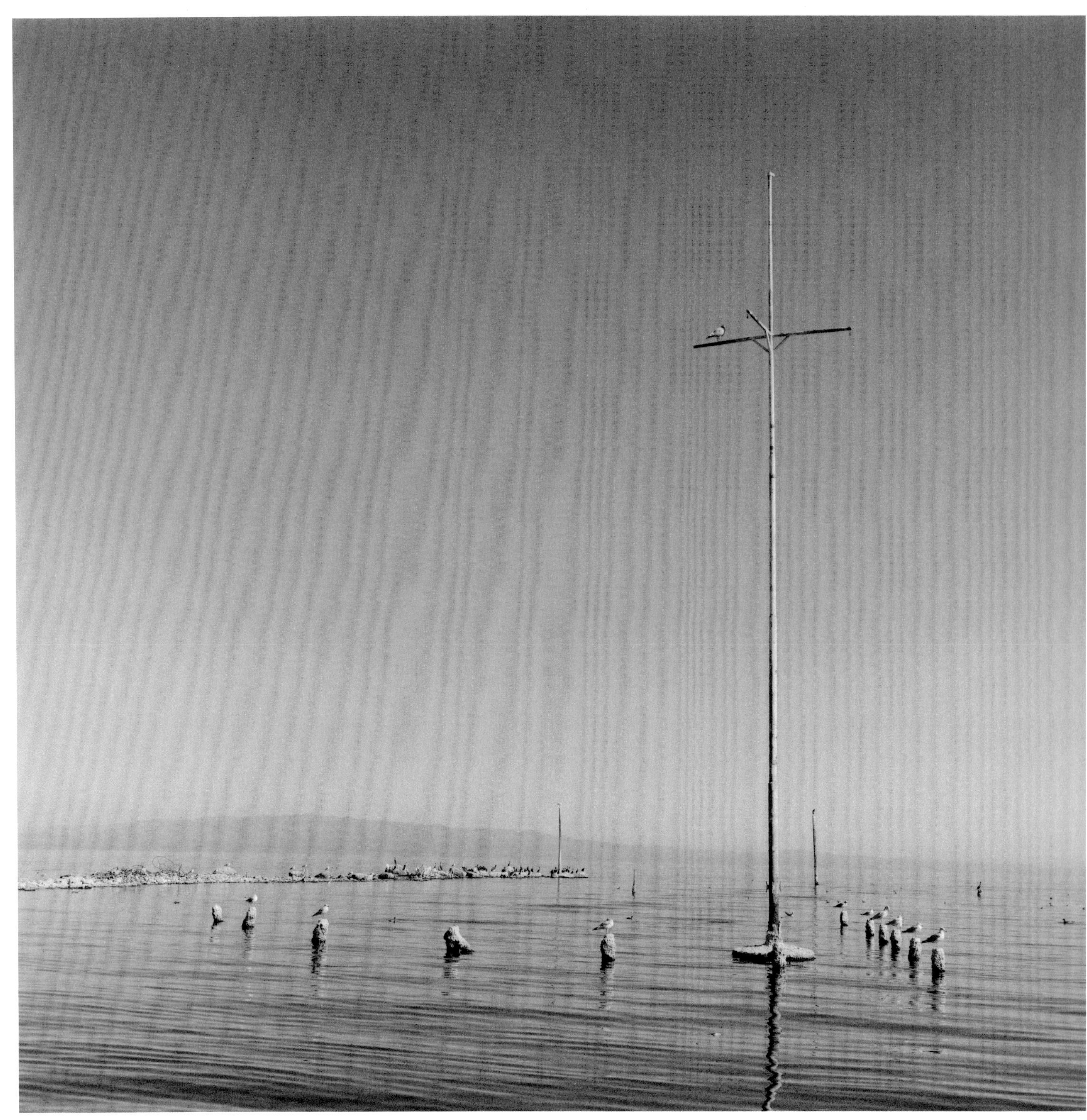

Marina
Salton Sea, California

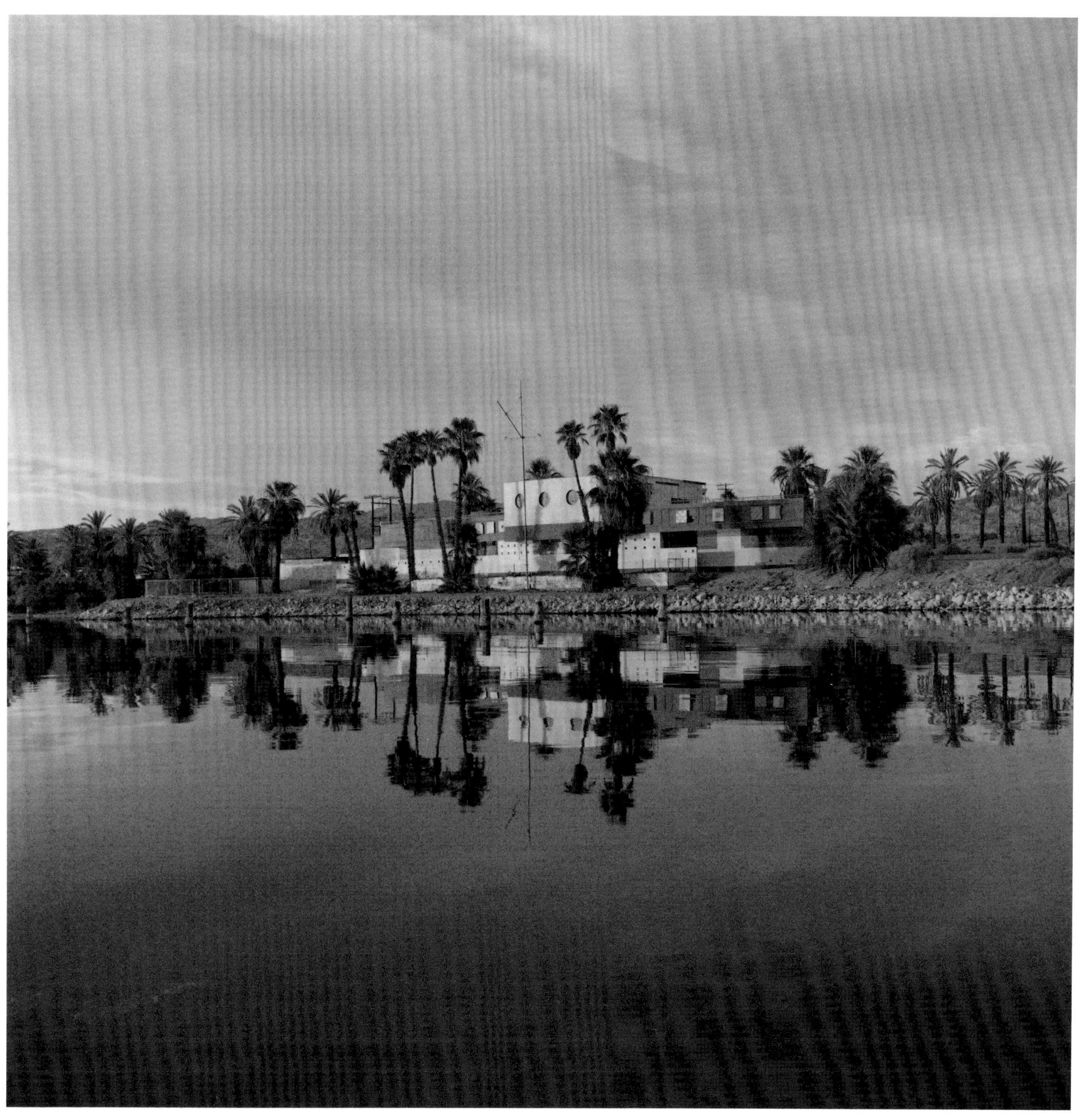

Abandoned Hotel
Salton Sea, California

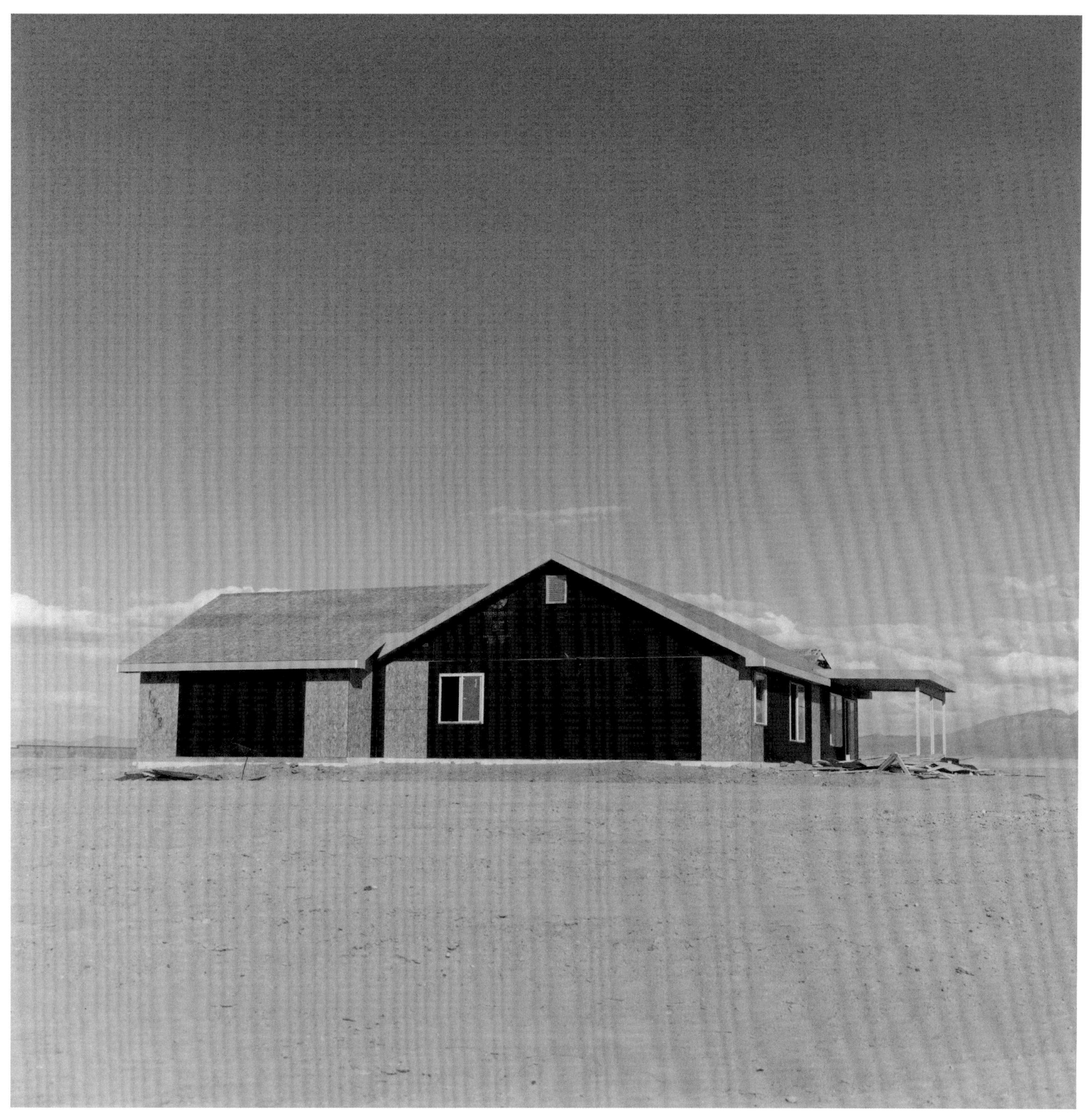

Construction Site
New Mexico

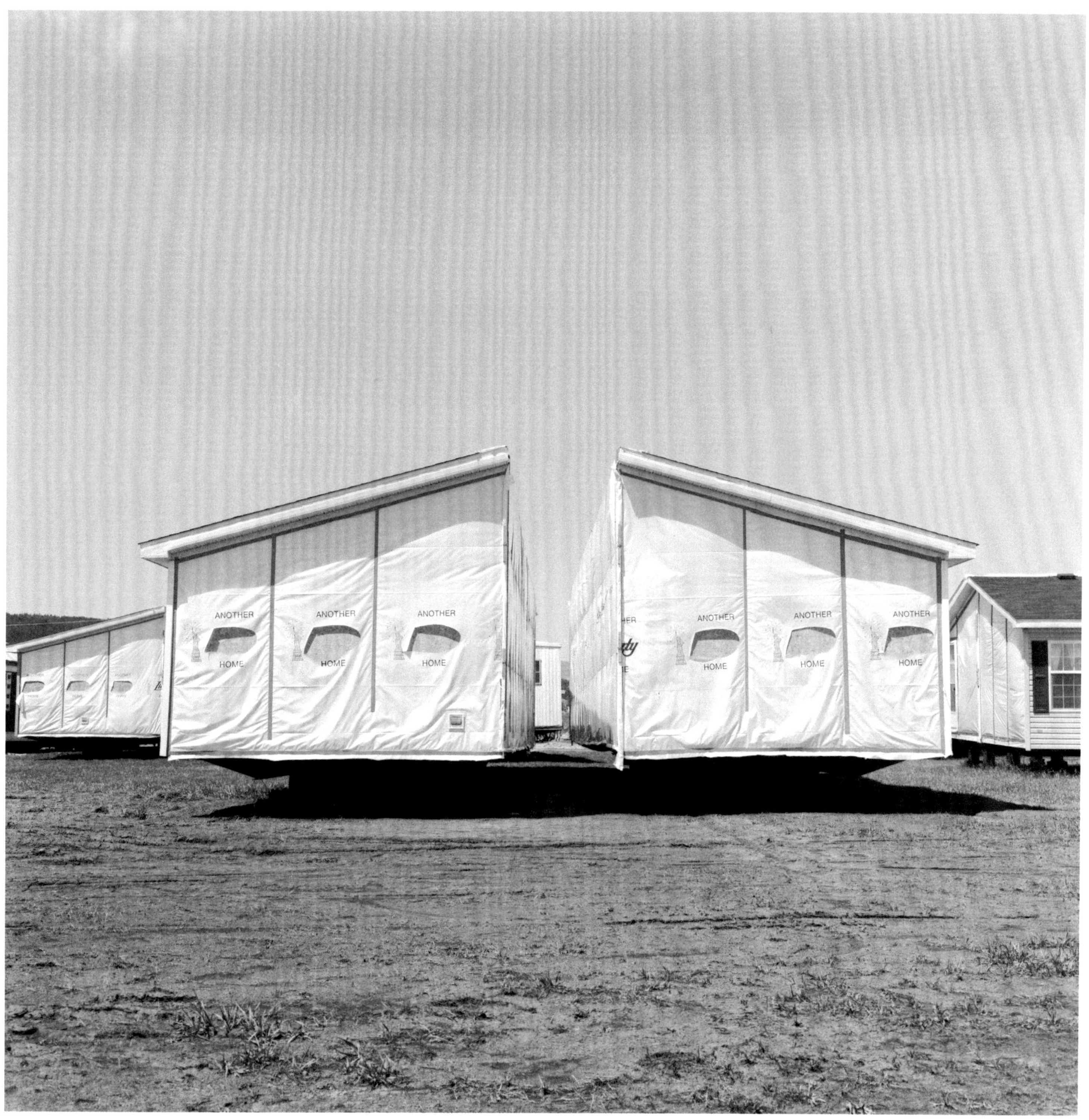

Prefabricated House
Great Plains, South Dakota

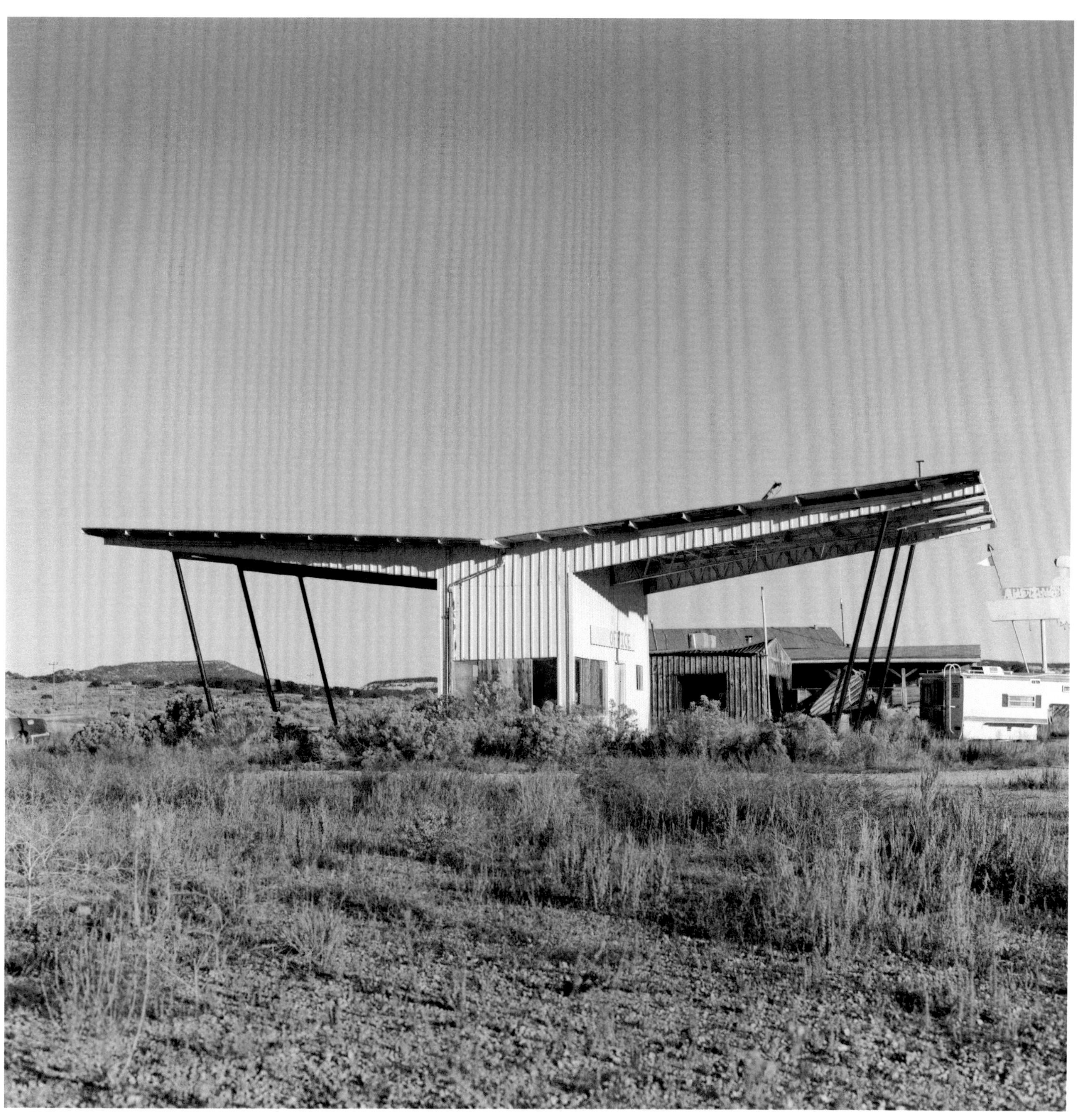

Abandoned Motel
Moab, Utah

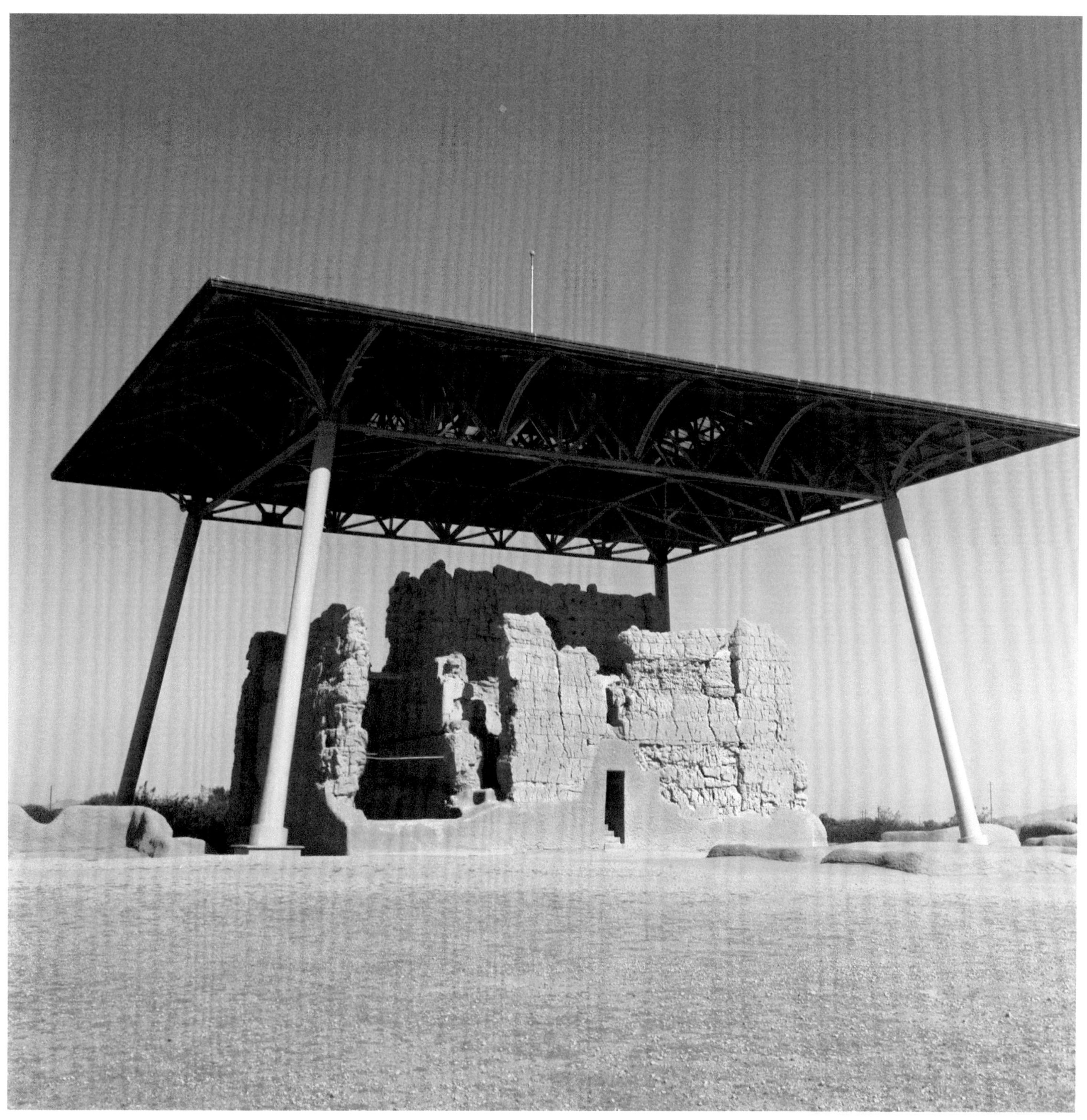

Casa Grande Monument
Arizona

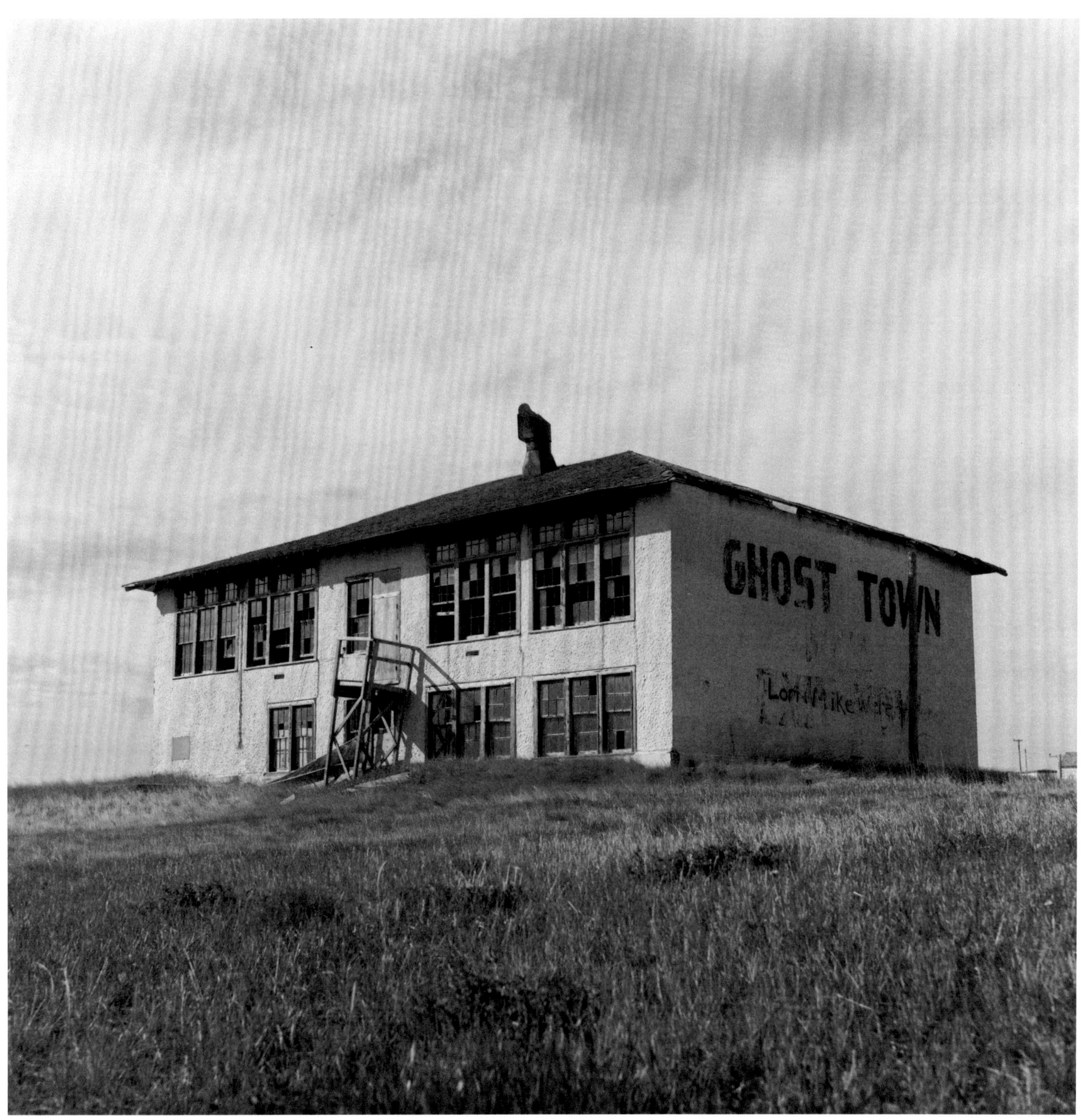

Ghost Town
Great Plains, South Dakota

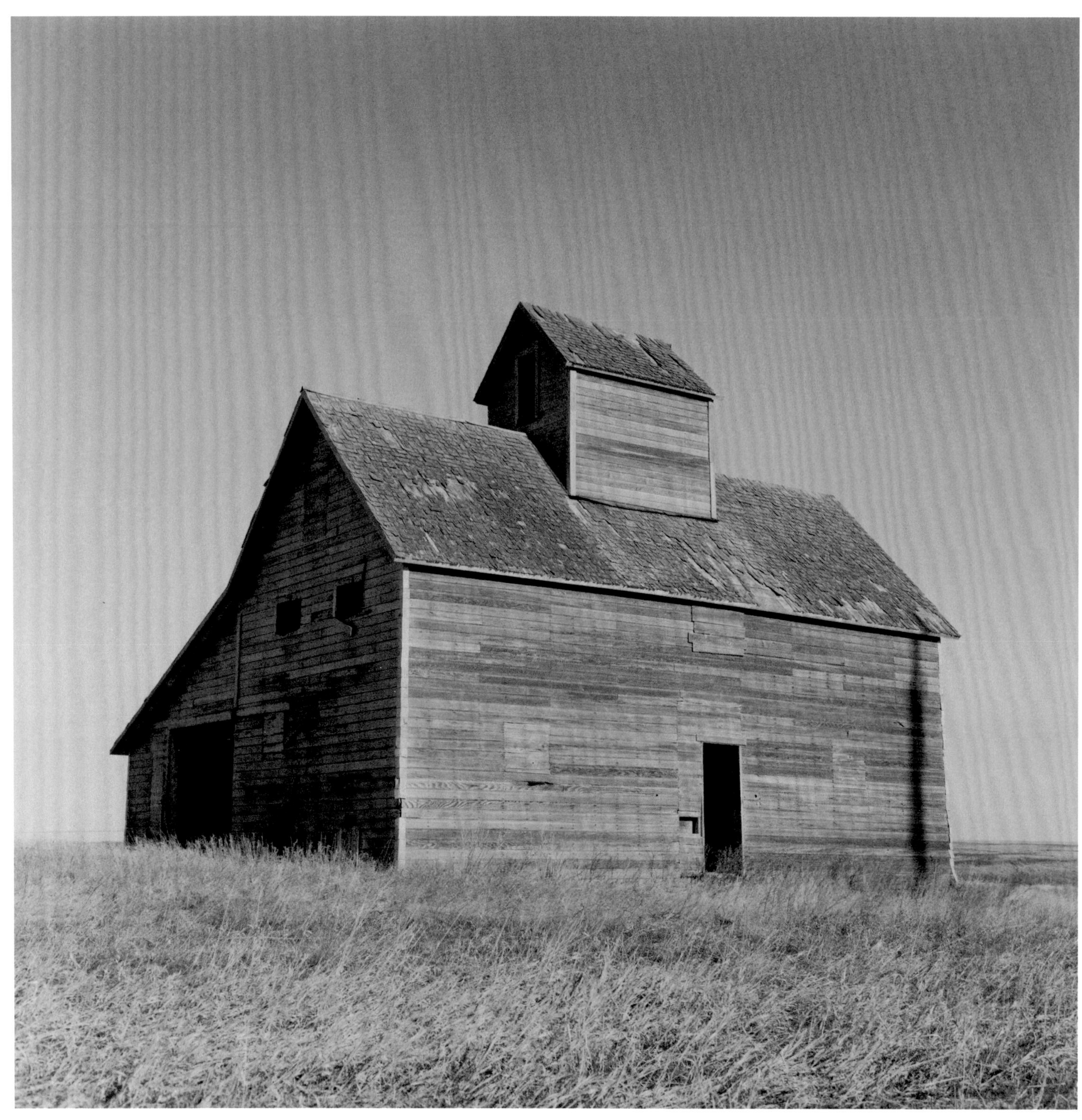

Barn
Great Plains, South Dakota

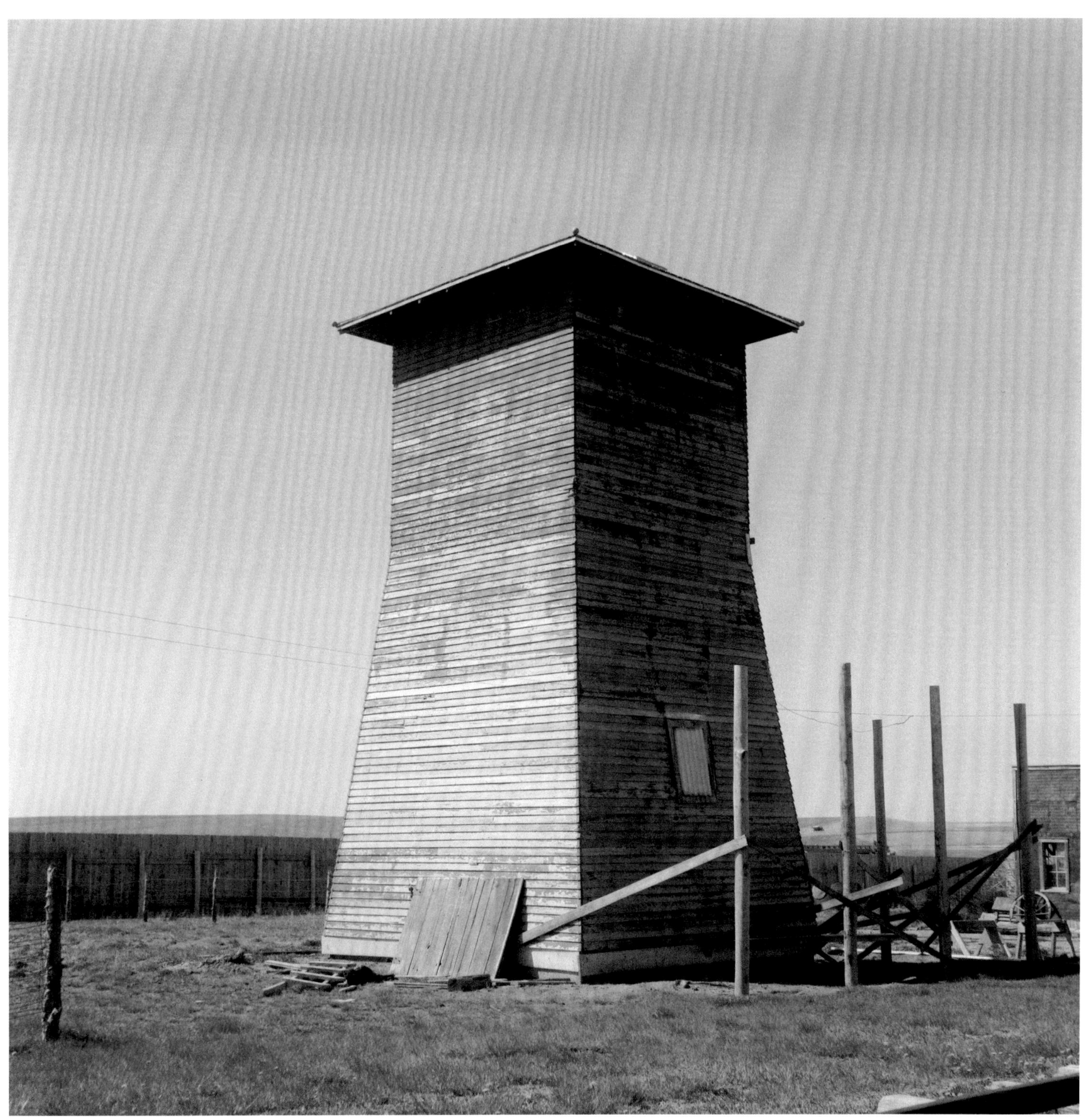

Grain Storage
Great Plains, South Dakota

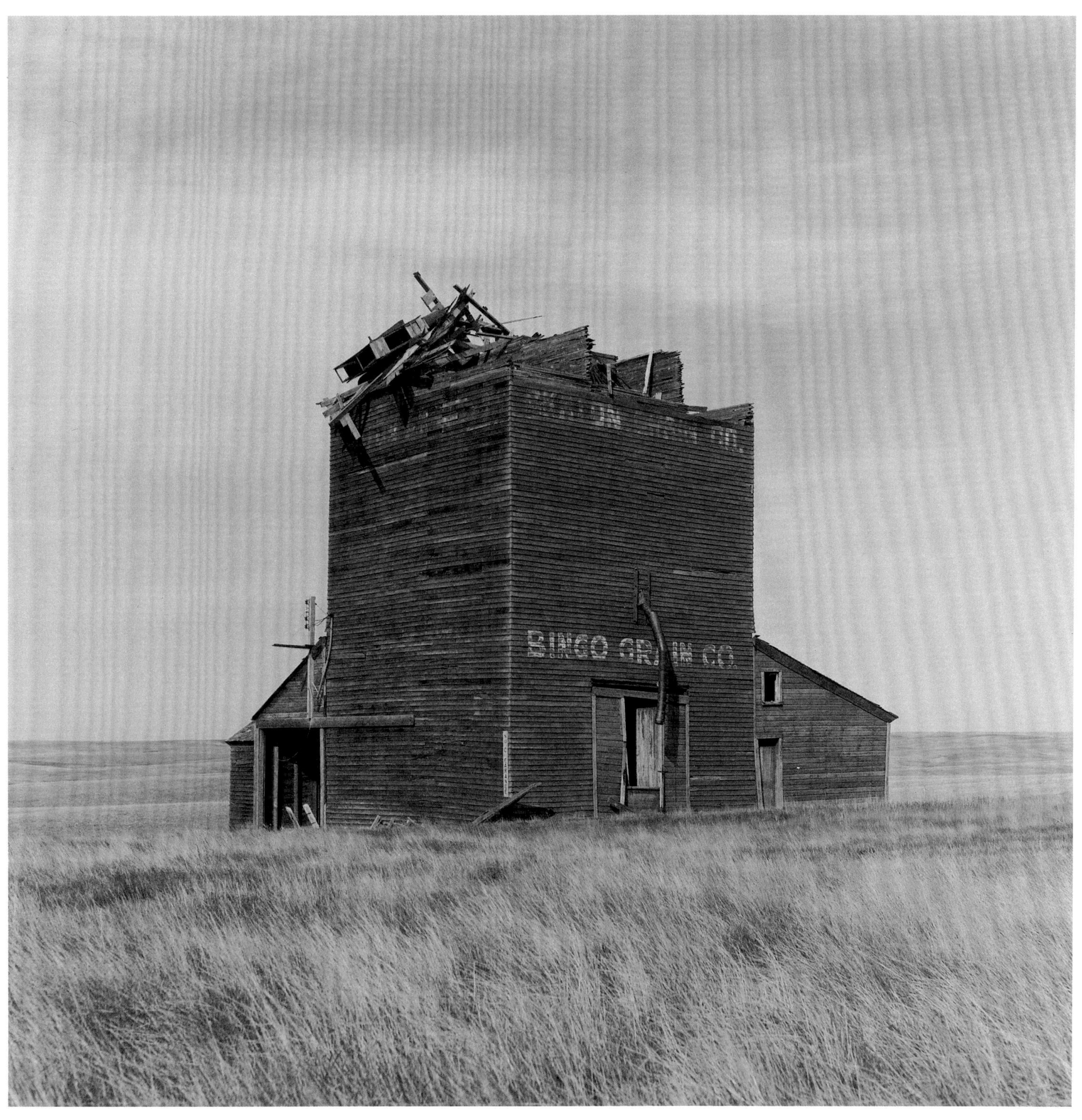

Bingo Grain Co.
Great Plains, South Dakota

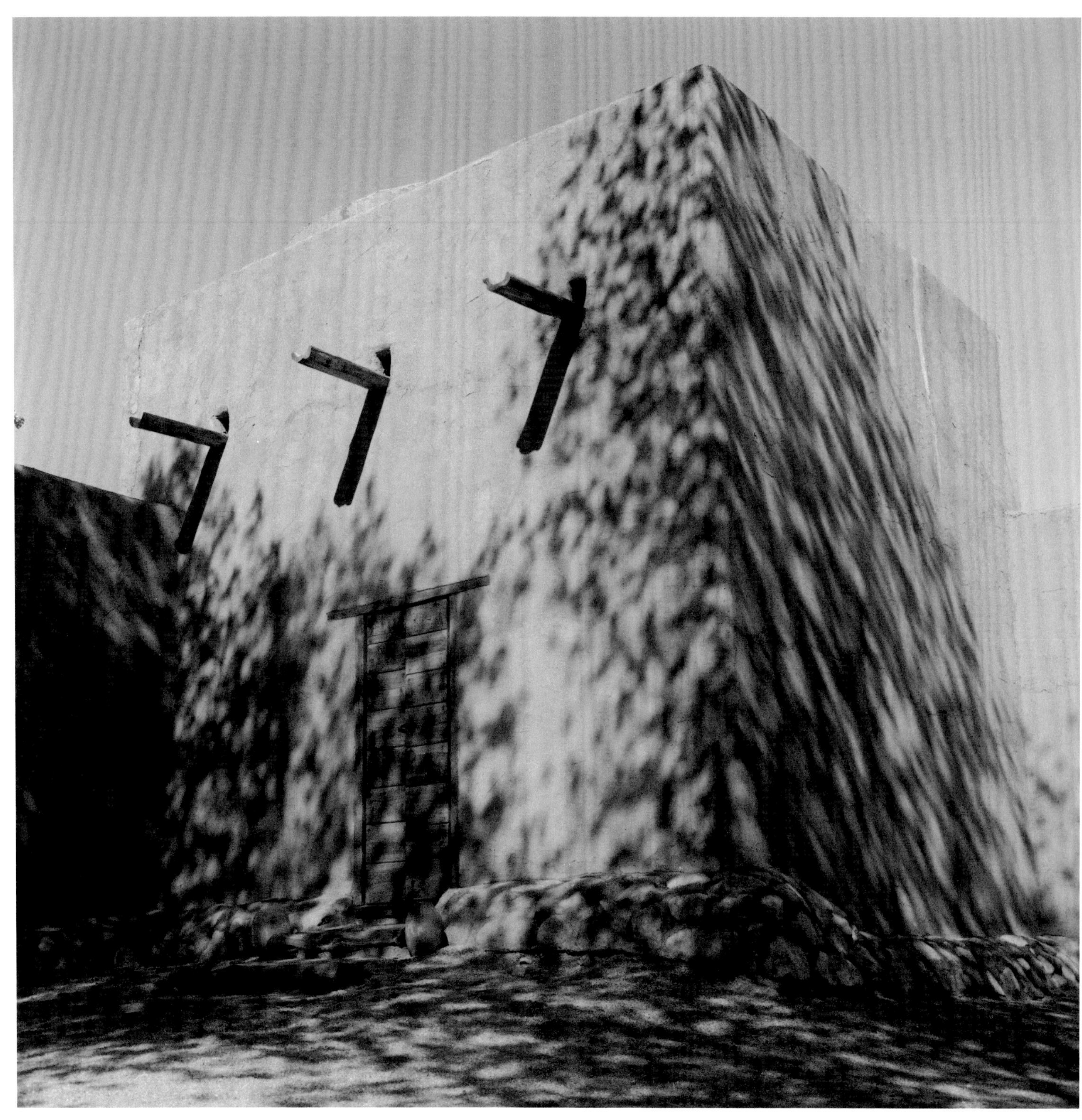

Cibolo Creek Ranch
Shafter, Texas

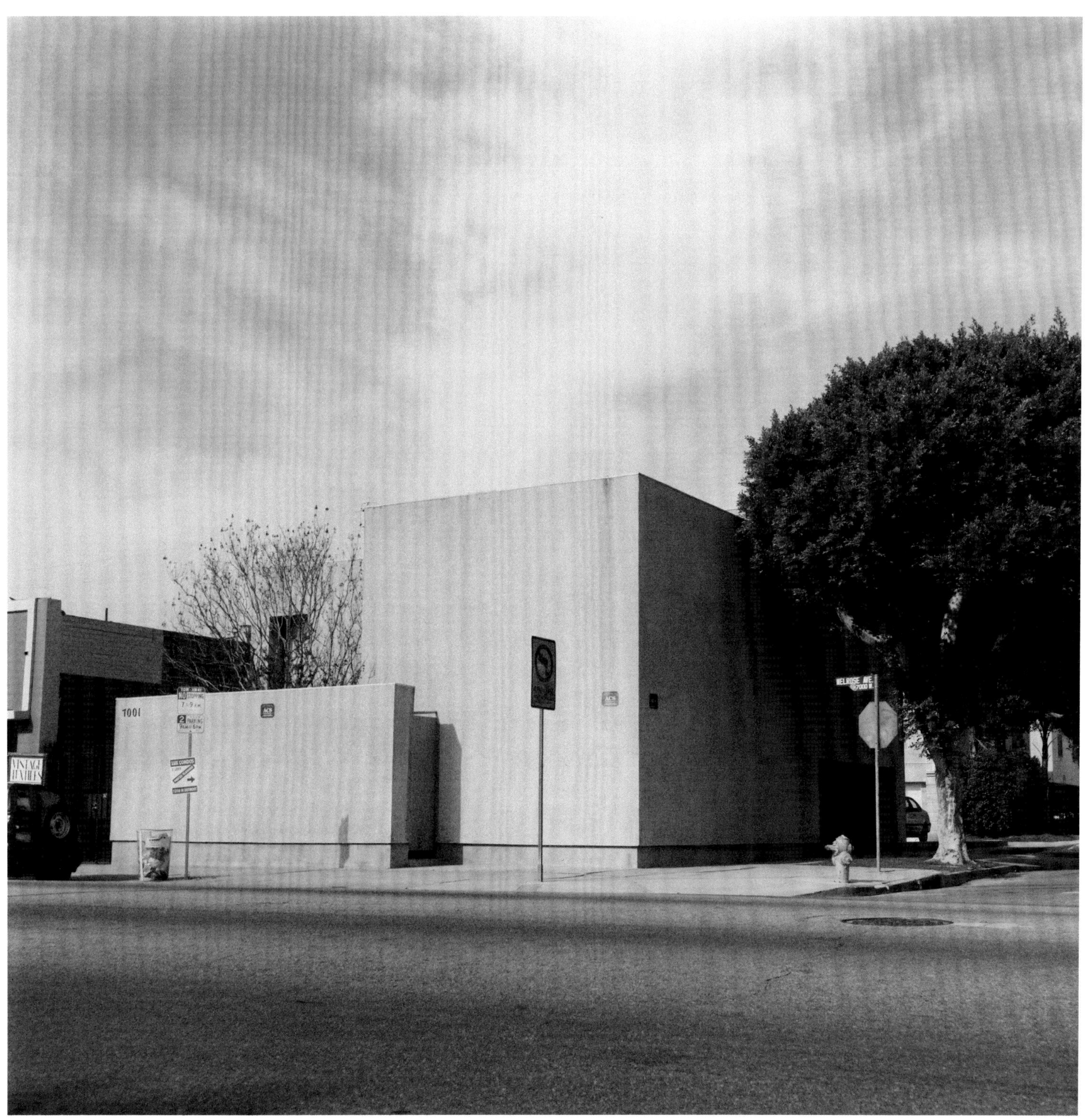

Danziger Studio
Frank O. Gehry, 1964–65 • Los Angeles, California

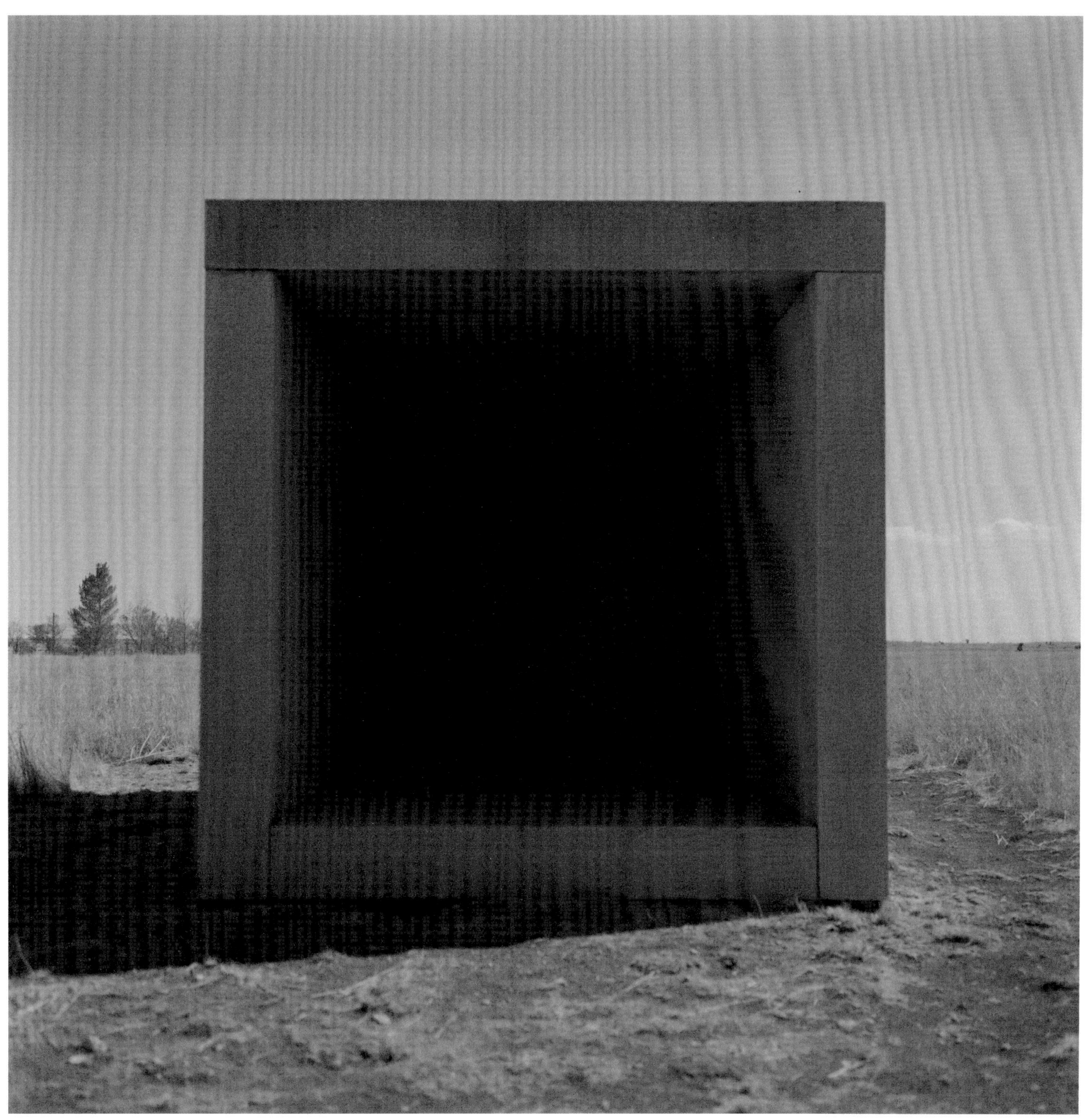

15 *Untitled Works in Concrete (detail), Chinati Foundation*
Donald Judd, 1980–84 • Marfa, Texas

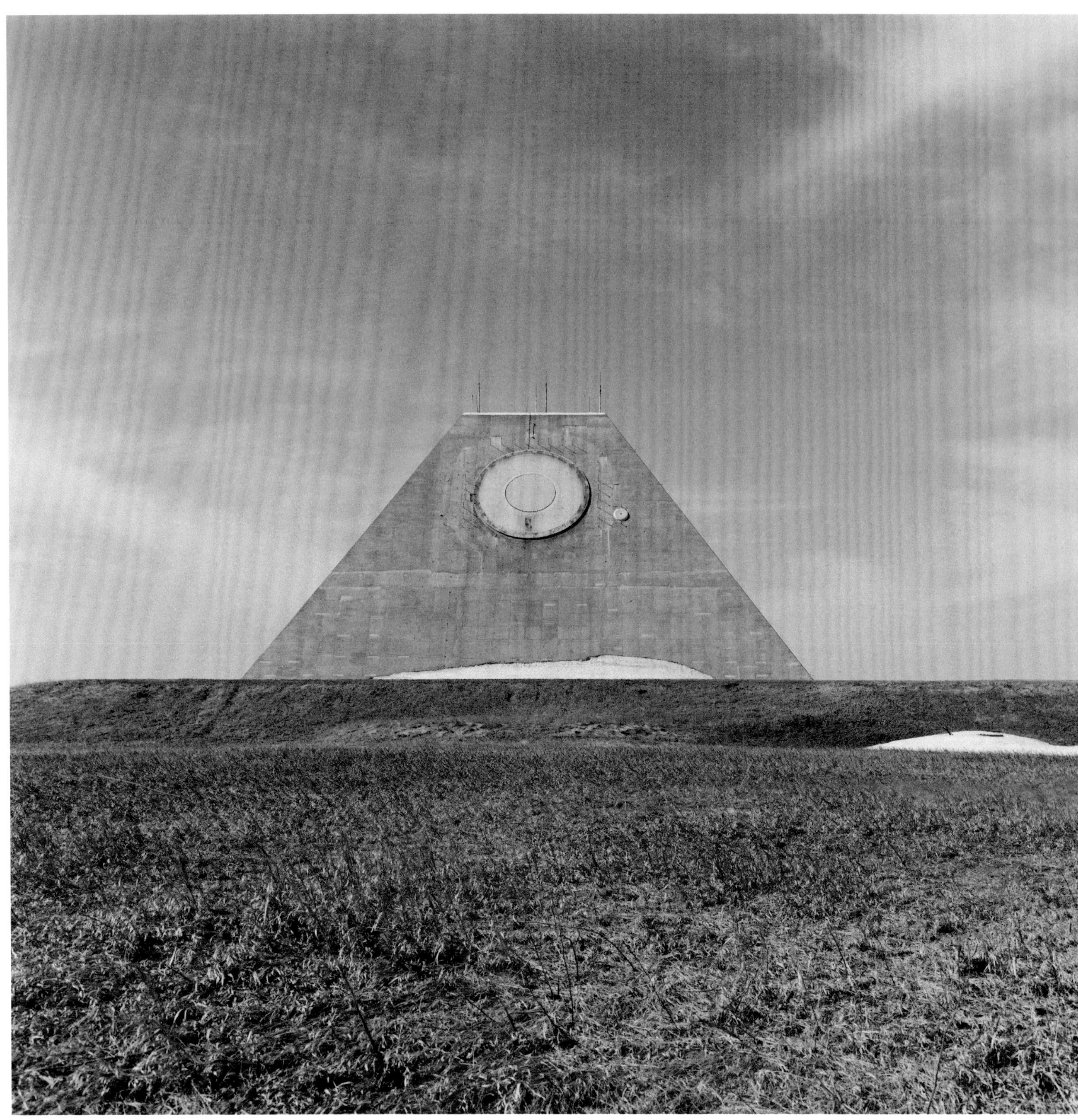

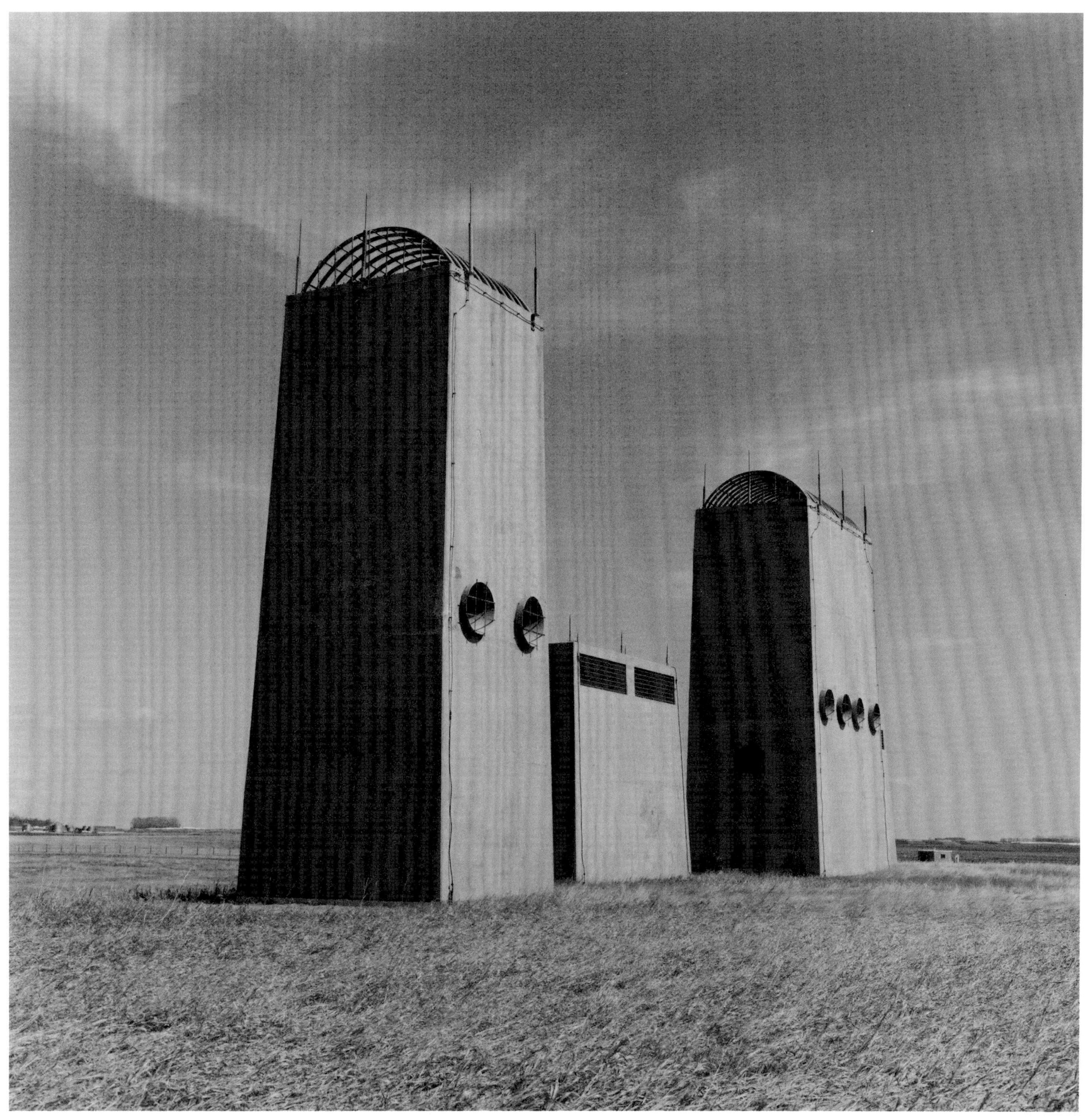

Stanley R. Mickelson Safeguard Antiballistic Missile Complex
1976 • Nekoma, North Dakota

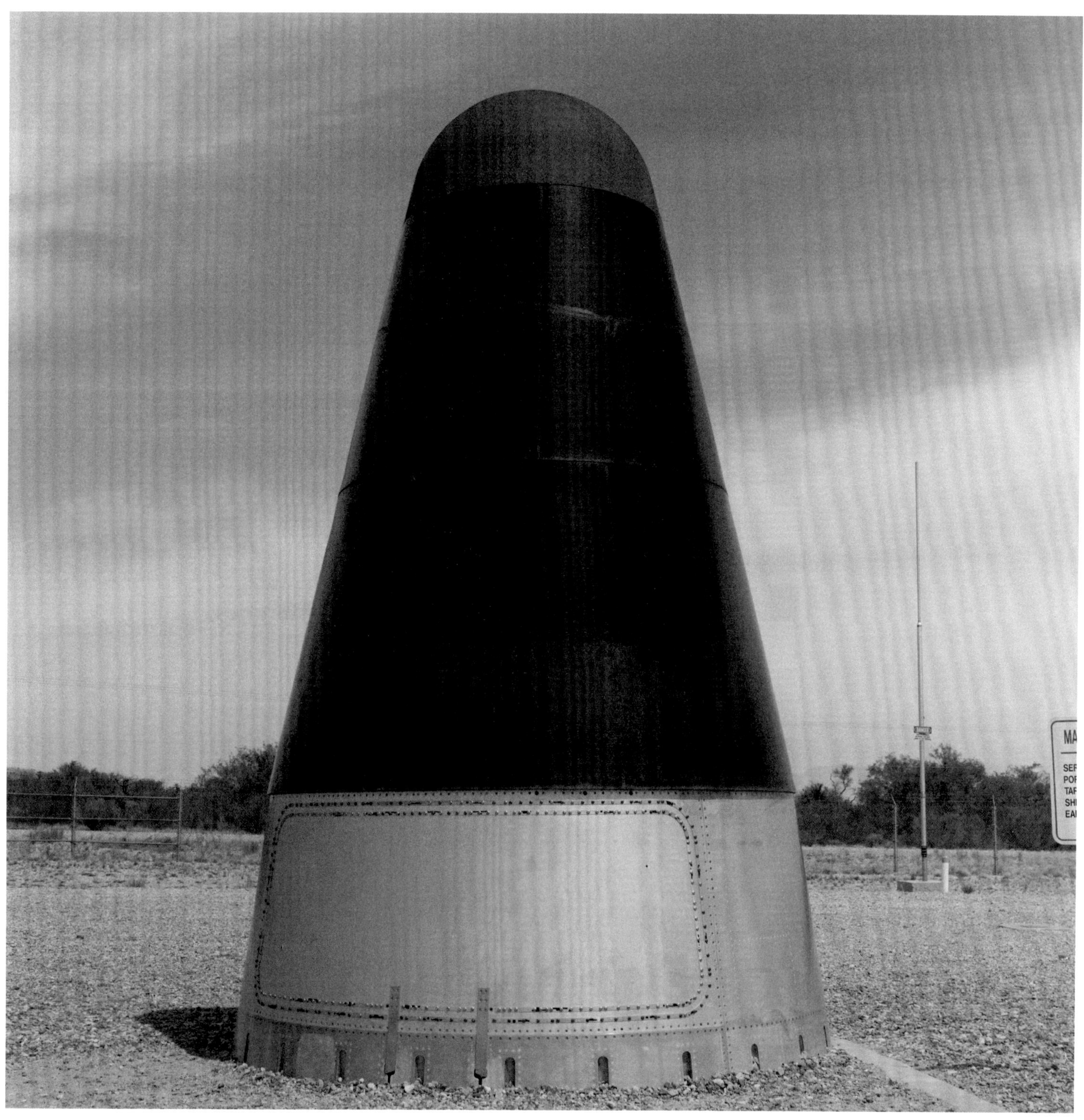

Missile Museum
Arizona

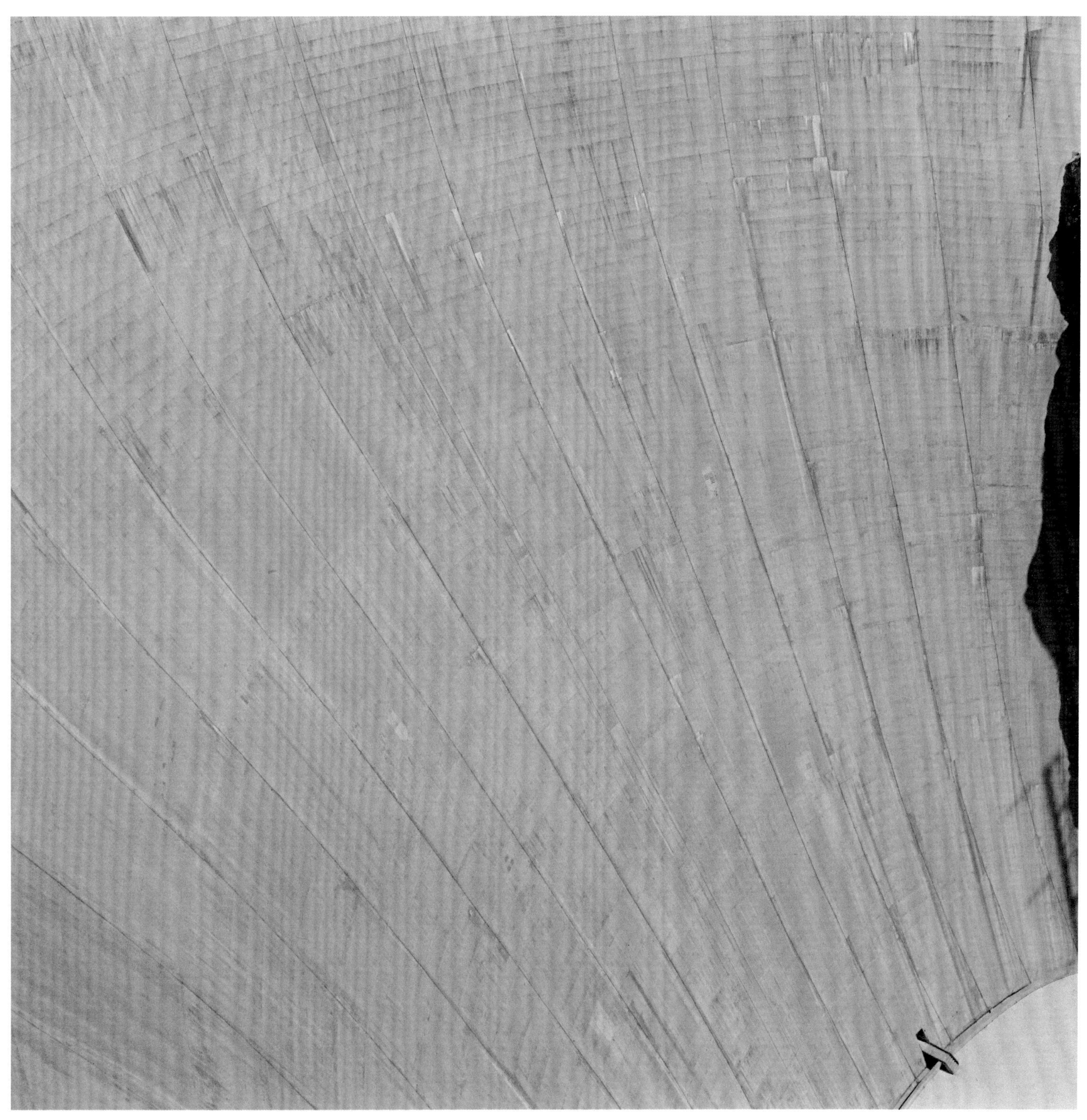

Hoover Dam
1935 • *Boulder City, Nevada*

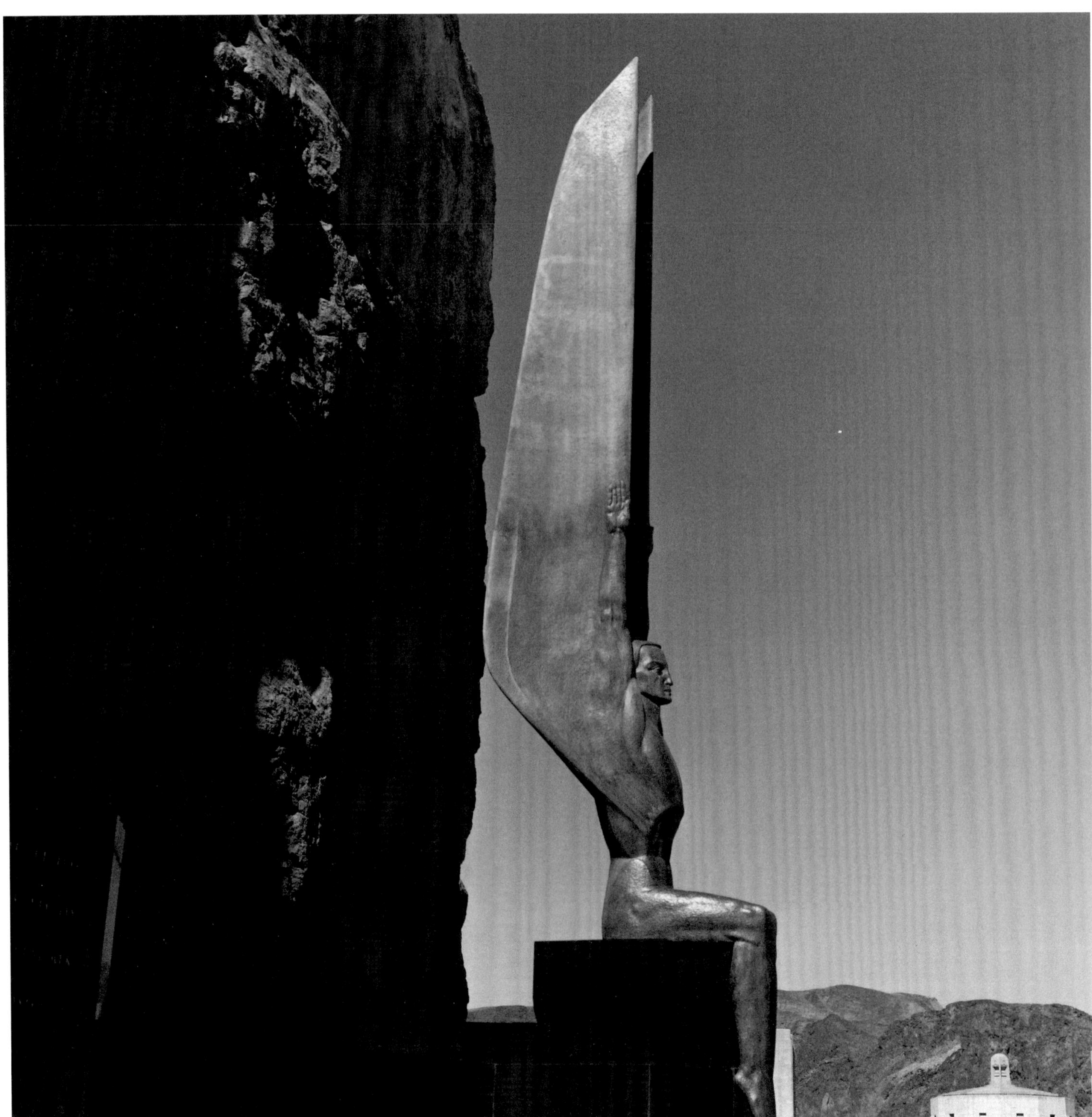

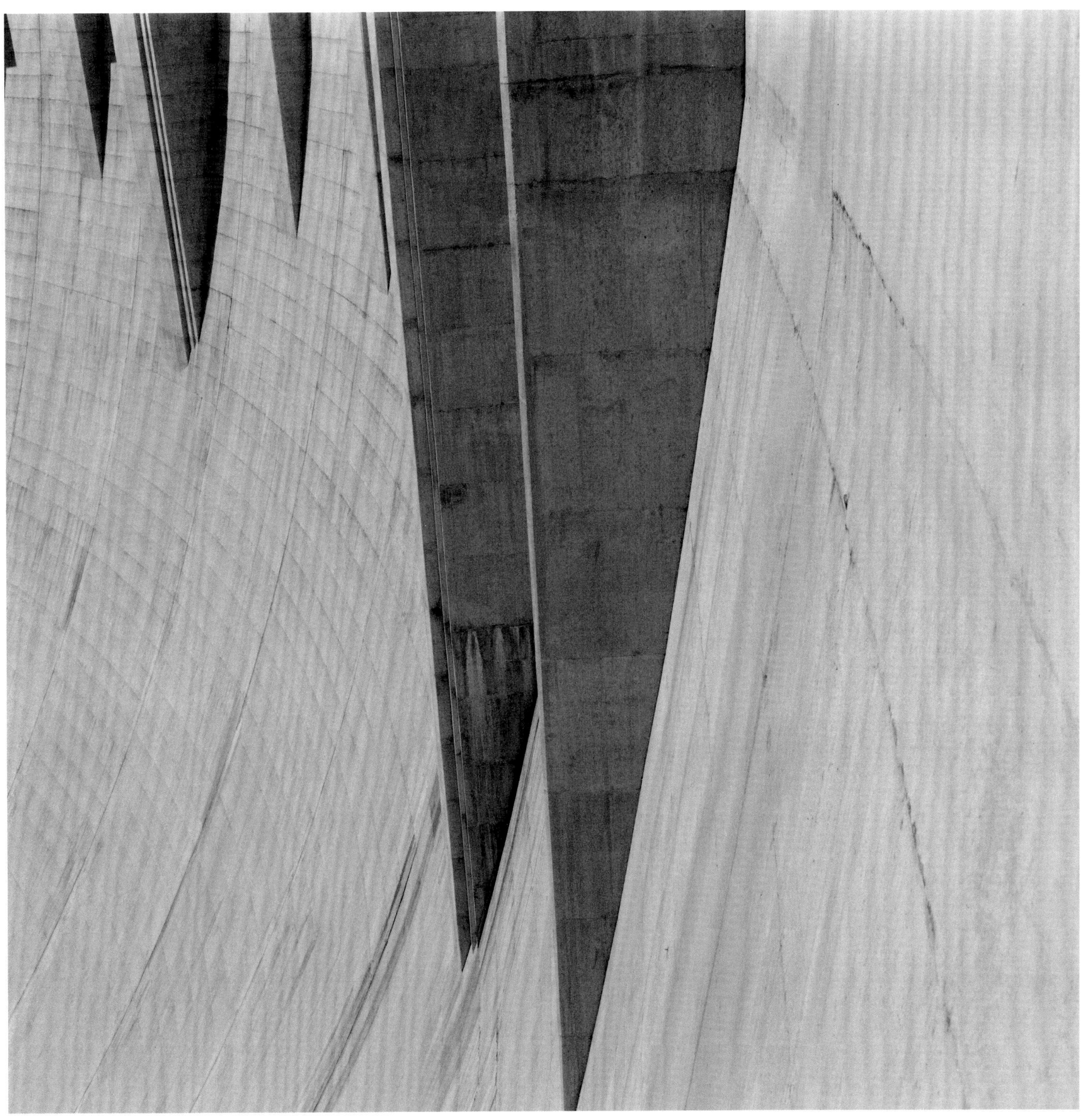

Hoover Dam
1935 · *Boulder City, Nevada*

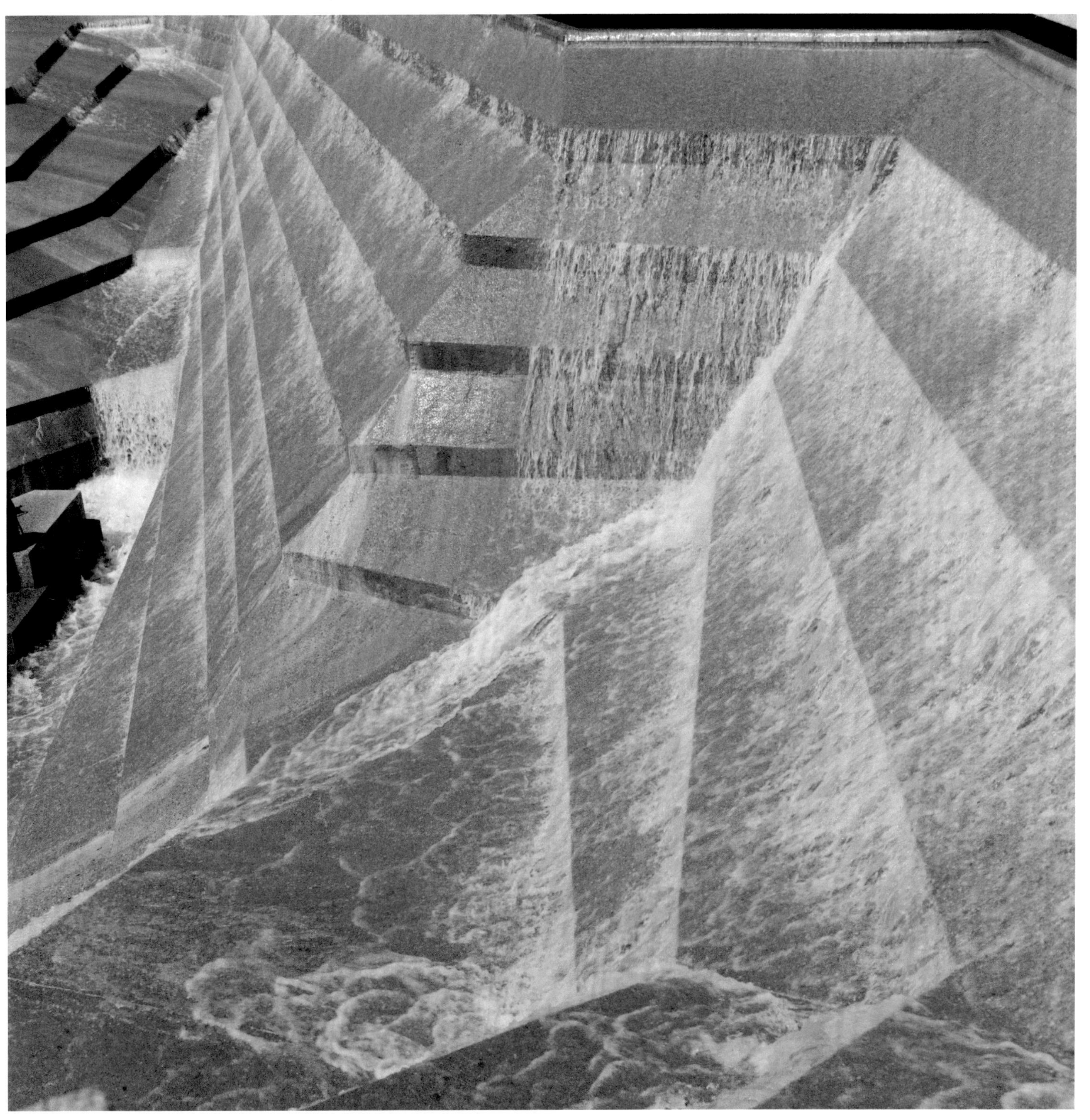

Water Garden
Johnson/Burgee Architects, 1974 • Fort Worth, Texas

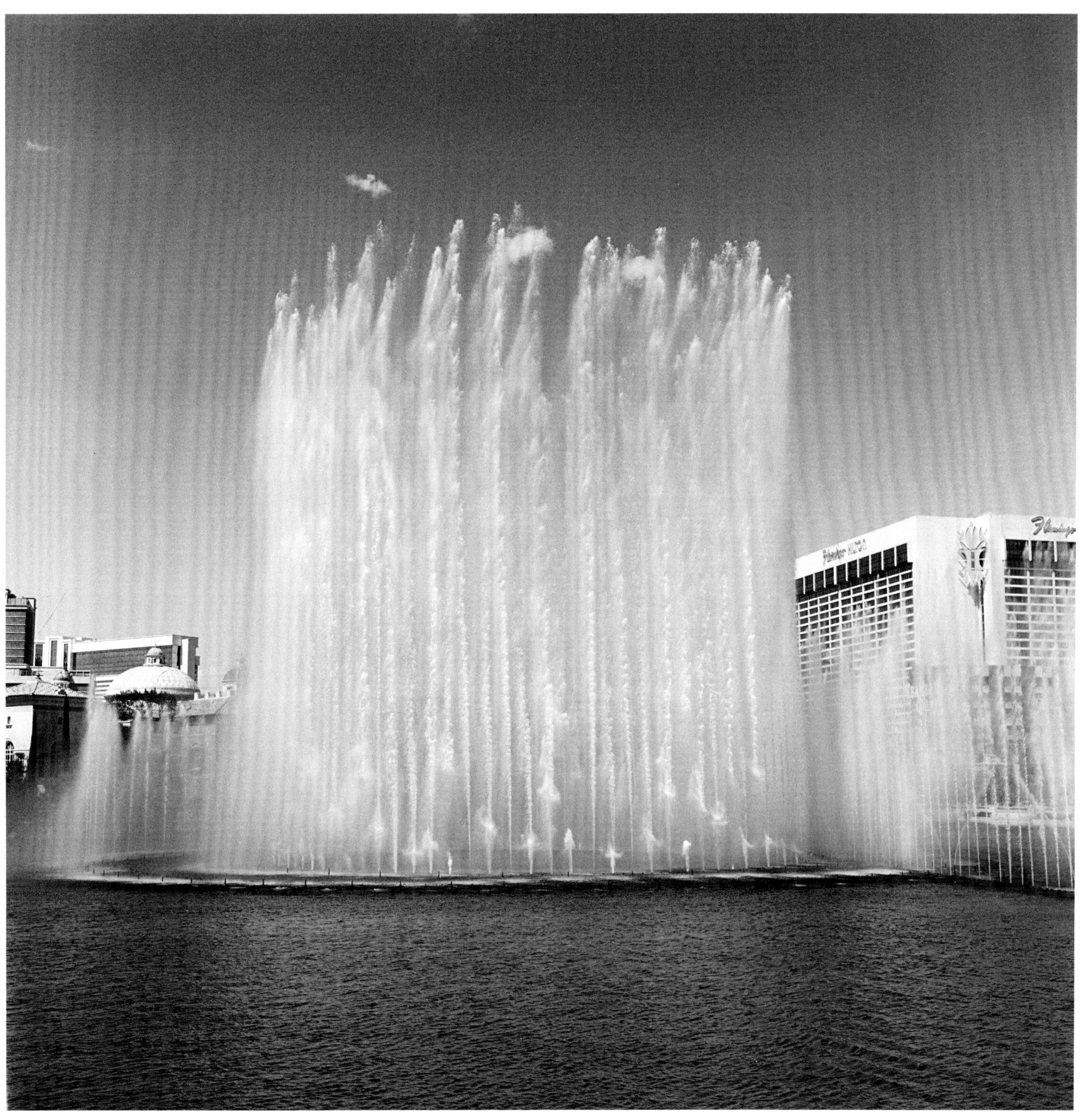

Dancing Waters
Las Vegas, Nevada

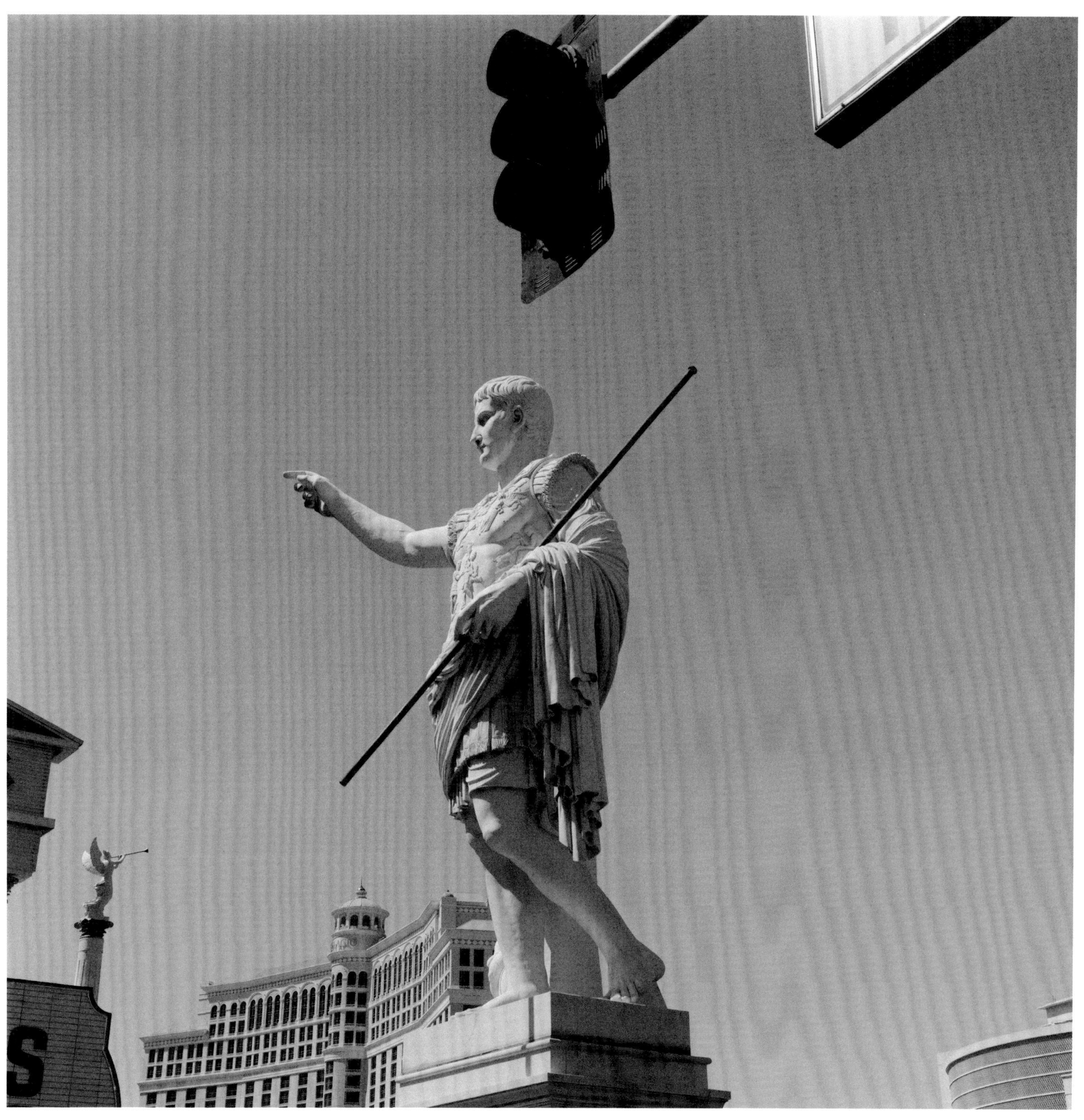

Caesars Palace
1966 • Las Vegas, Nevada

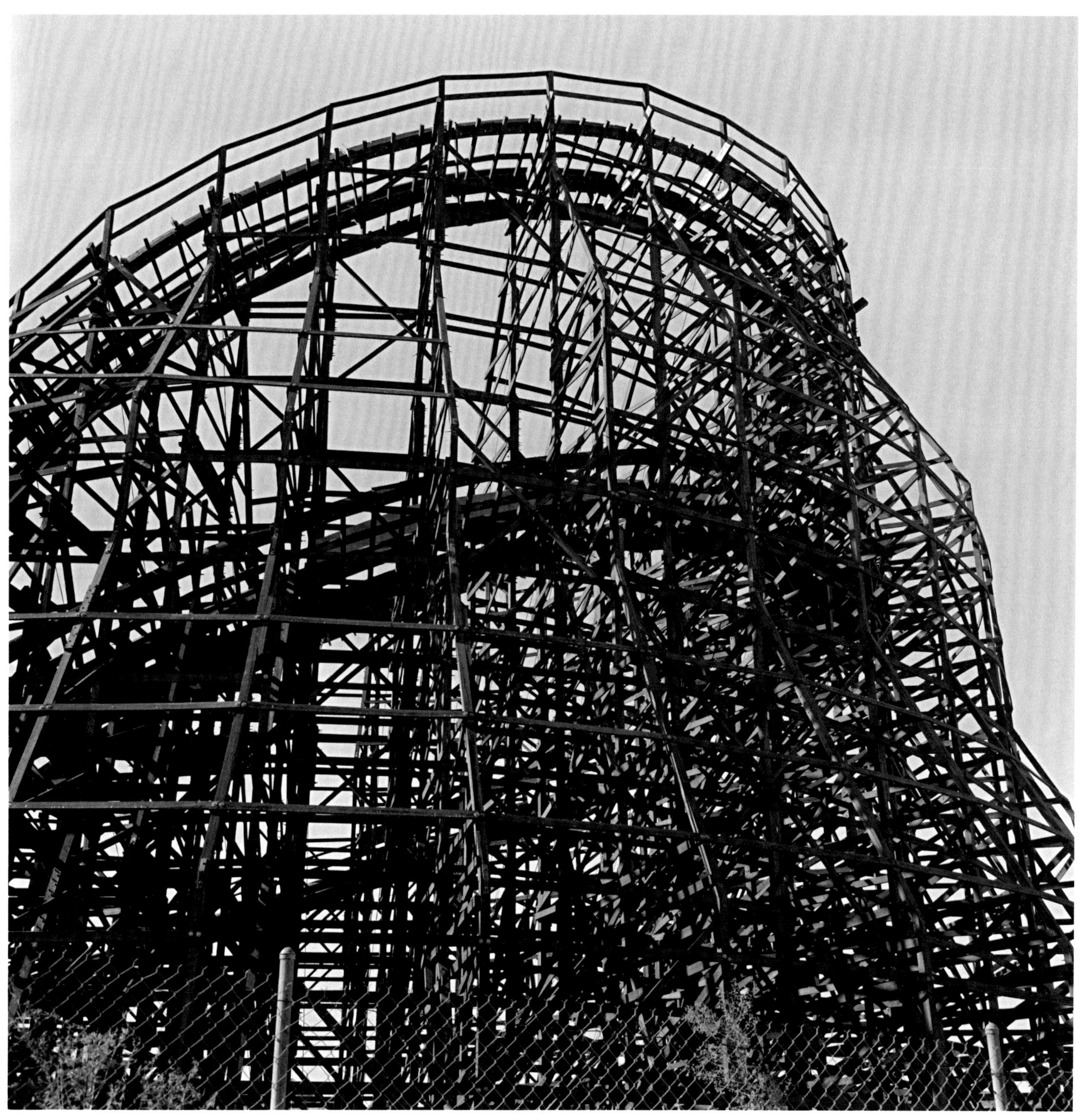

Psyclone, Six Flags Magic Mountain
Valencia, California

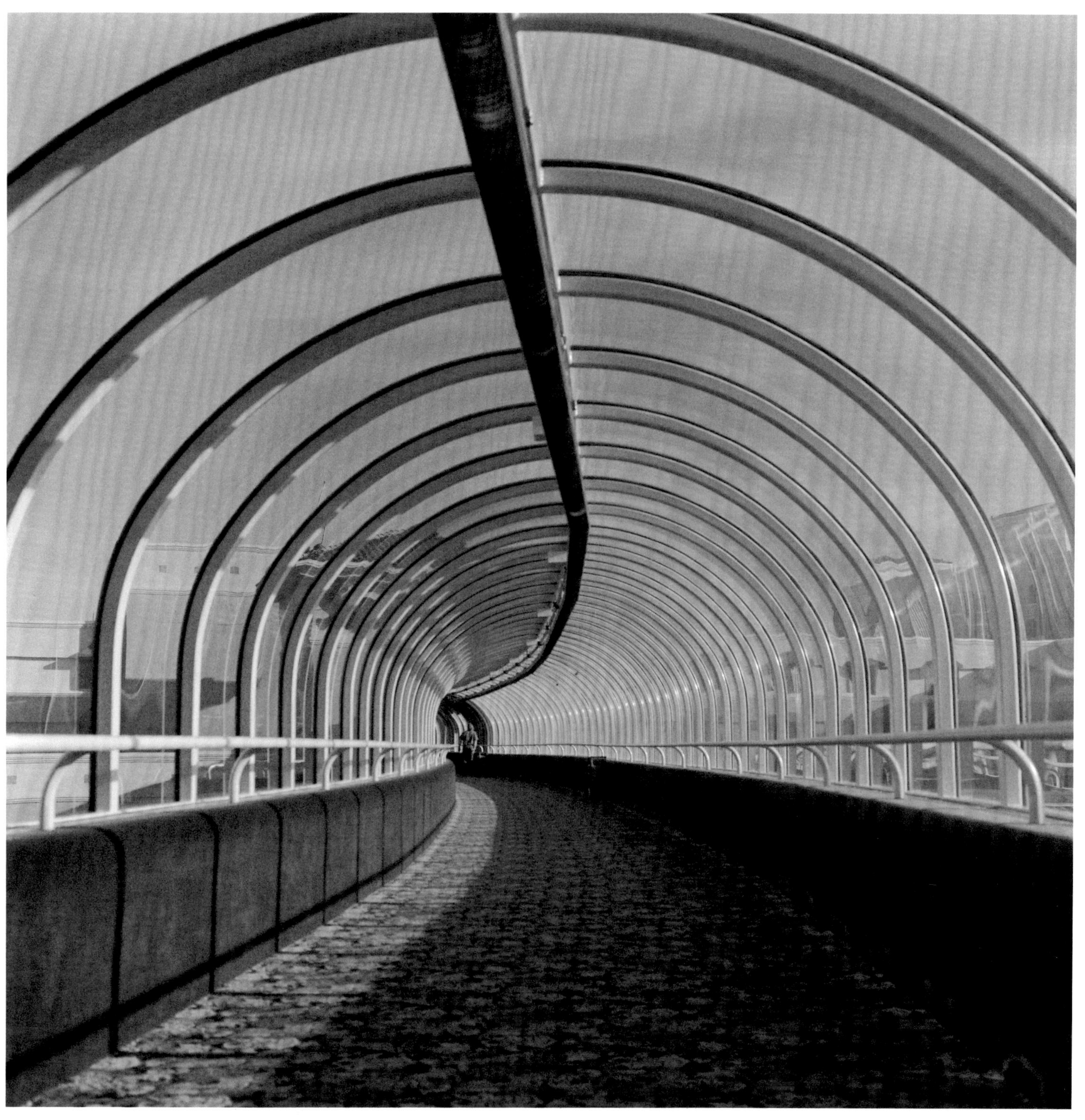

Hotel Passageway
State Line, Utah

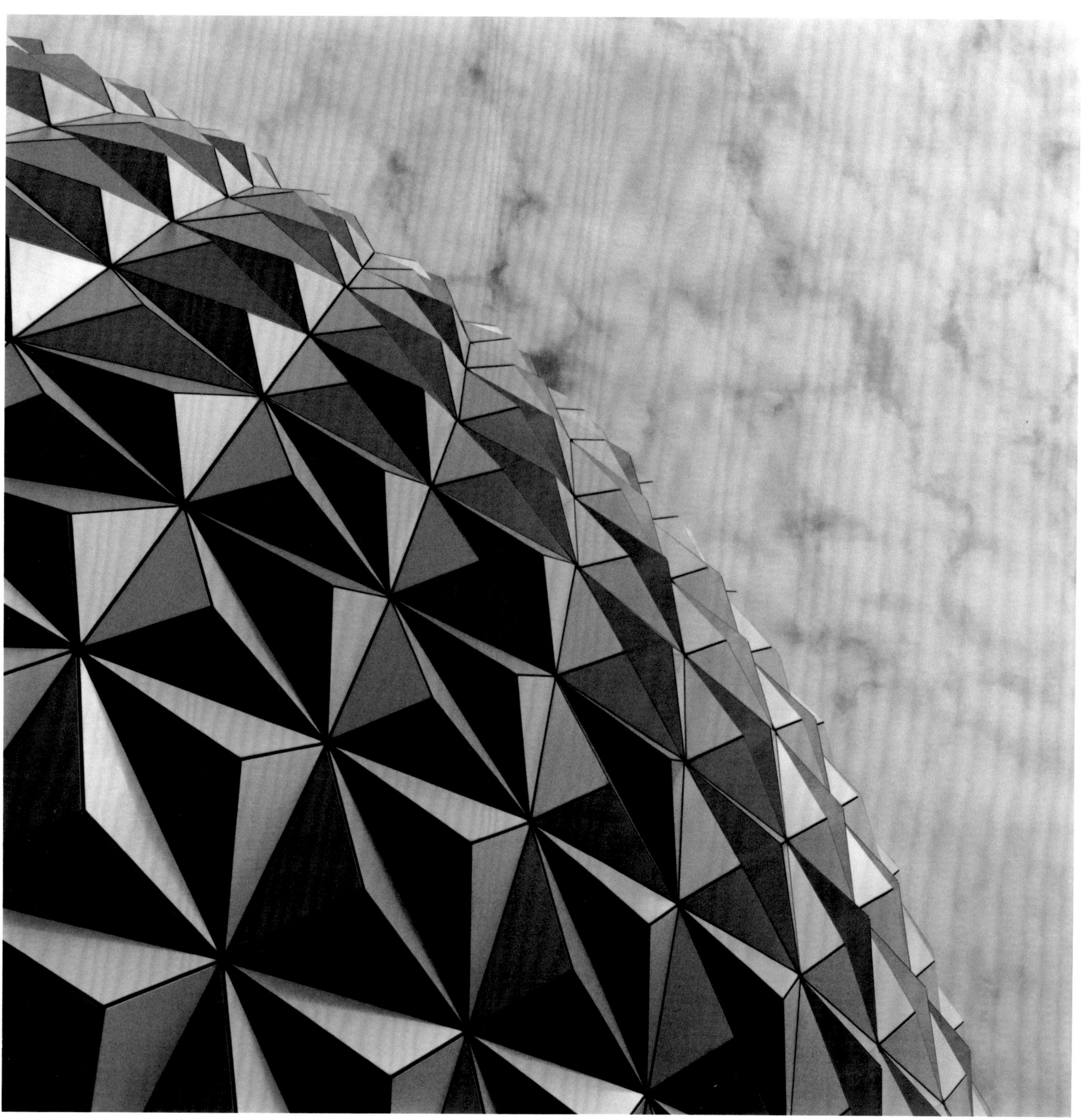

Spaceship Earth, Epcot, Walt Disney World
Lake Buena Vista, Florida

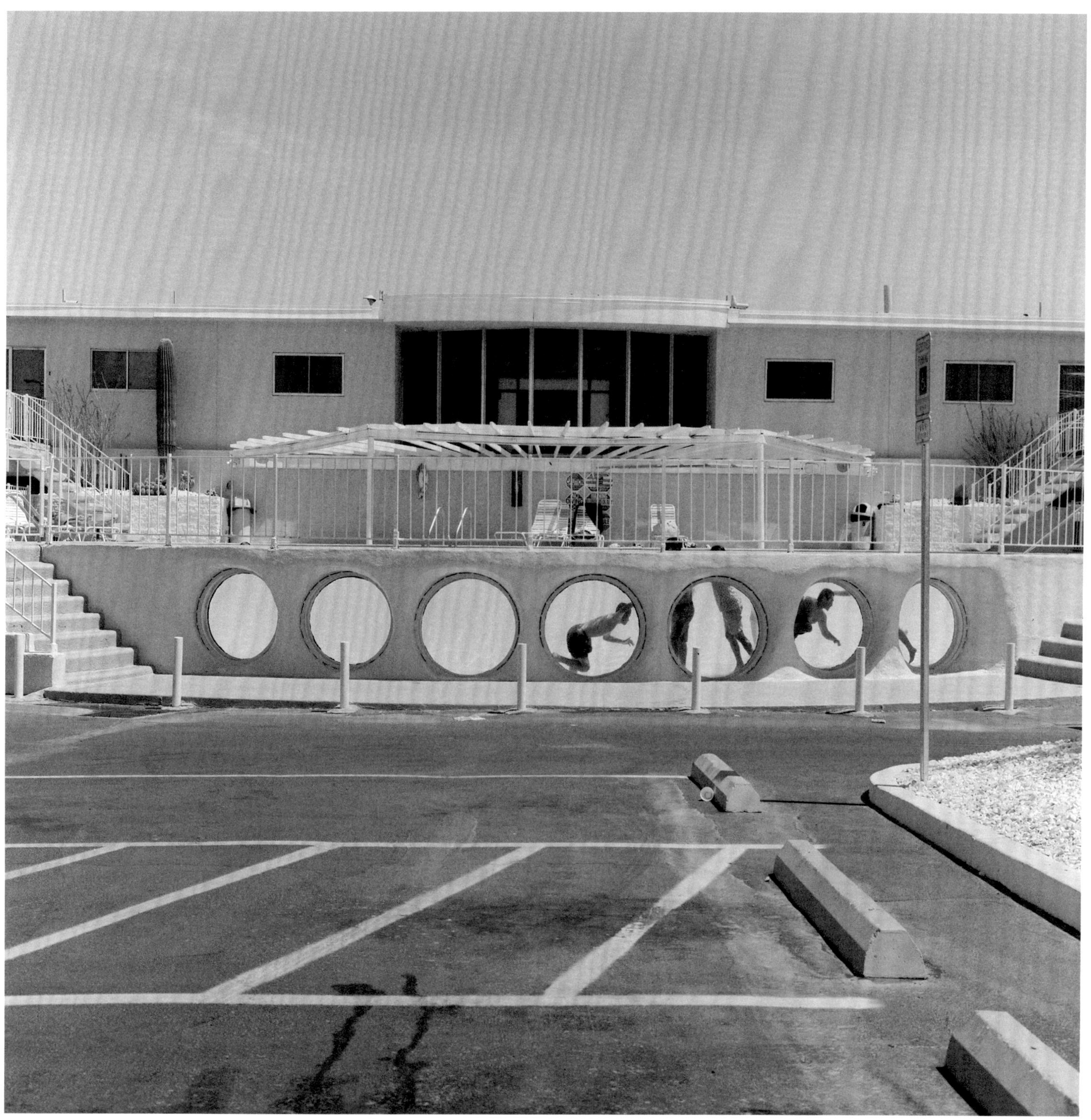

Hotel Swimming Pool
Las Vegas, Nevada

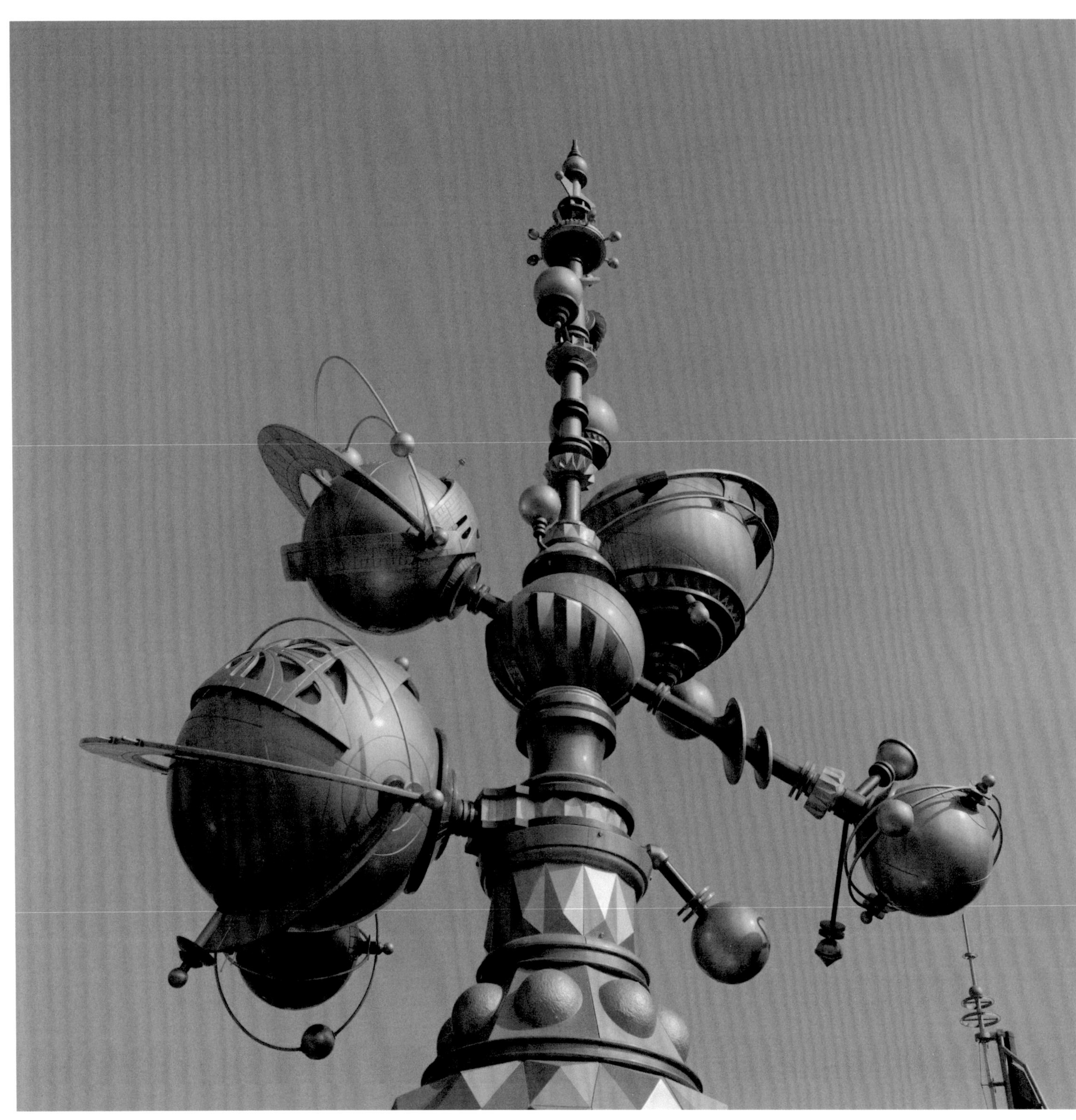

Astro Orbitor, Disneyland
Anaheim, California

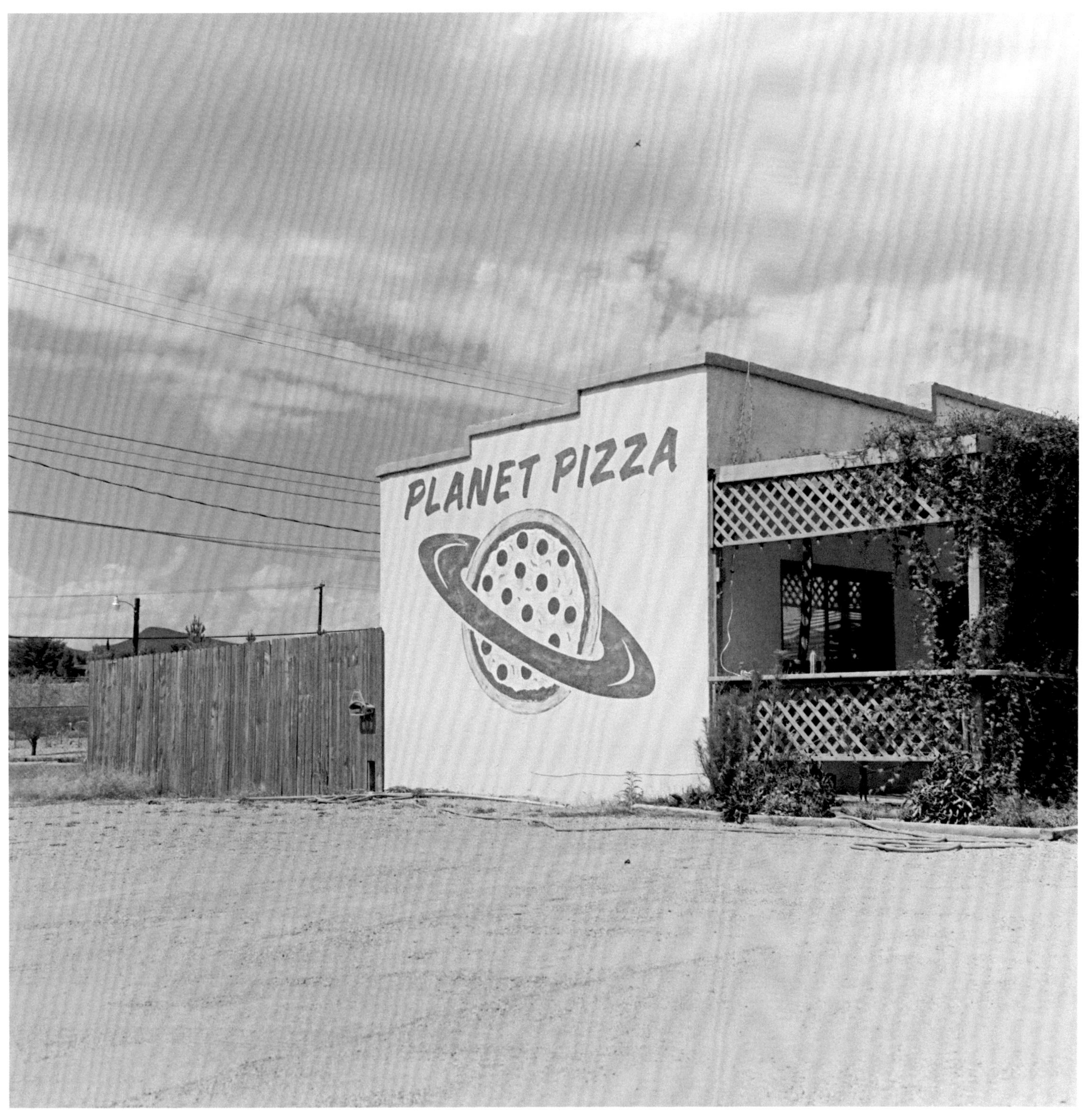

Planet Pizza
Truth or Consequences, New Mexico

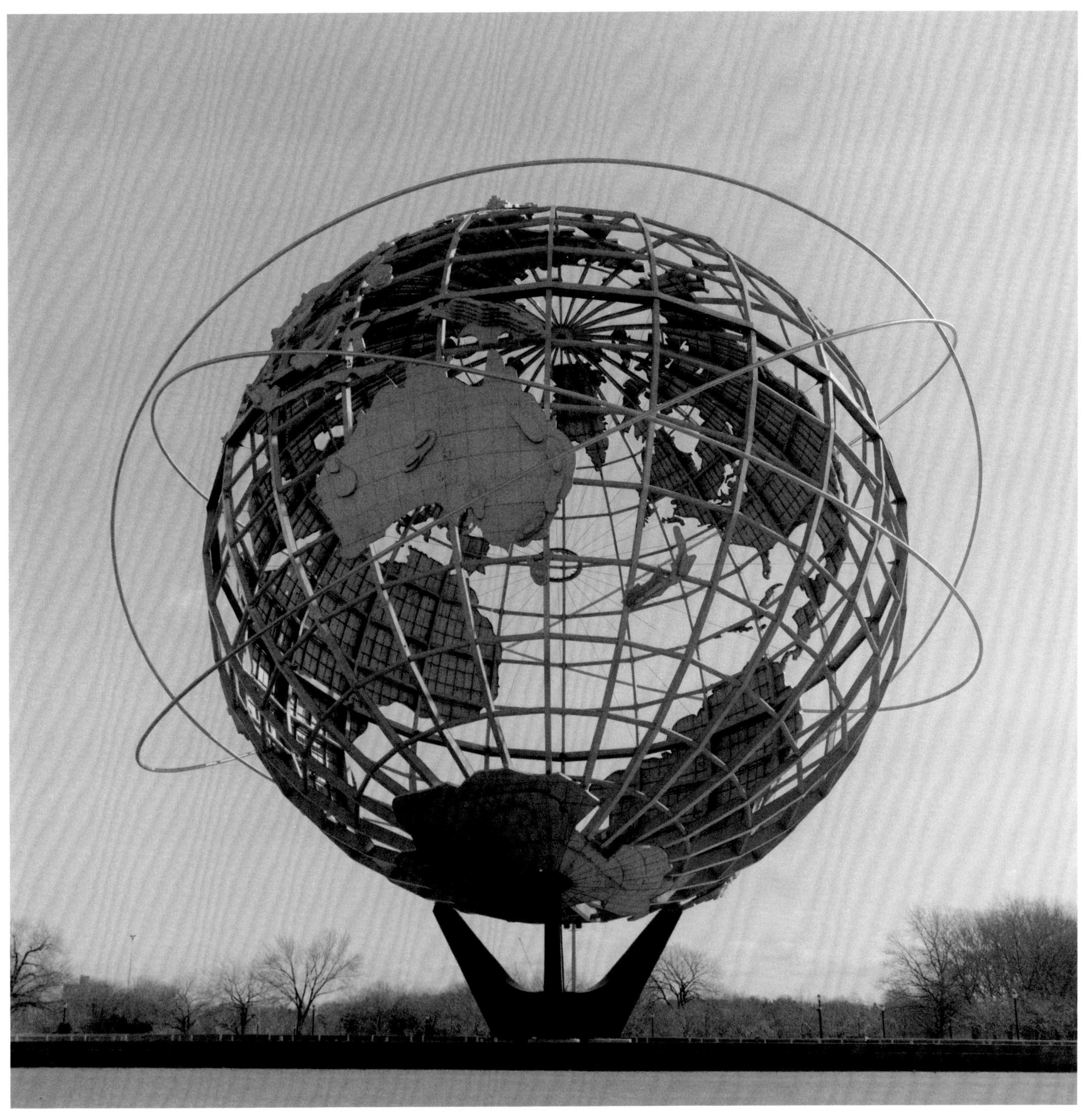

Unisphere
1964 · *Flushing, Queens*

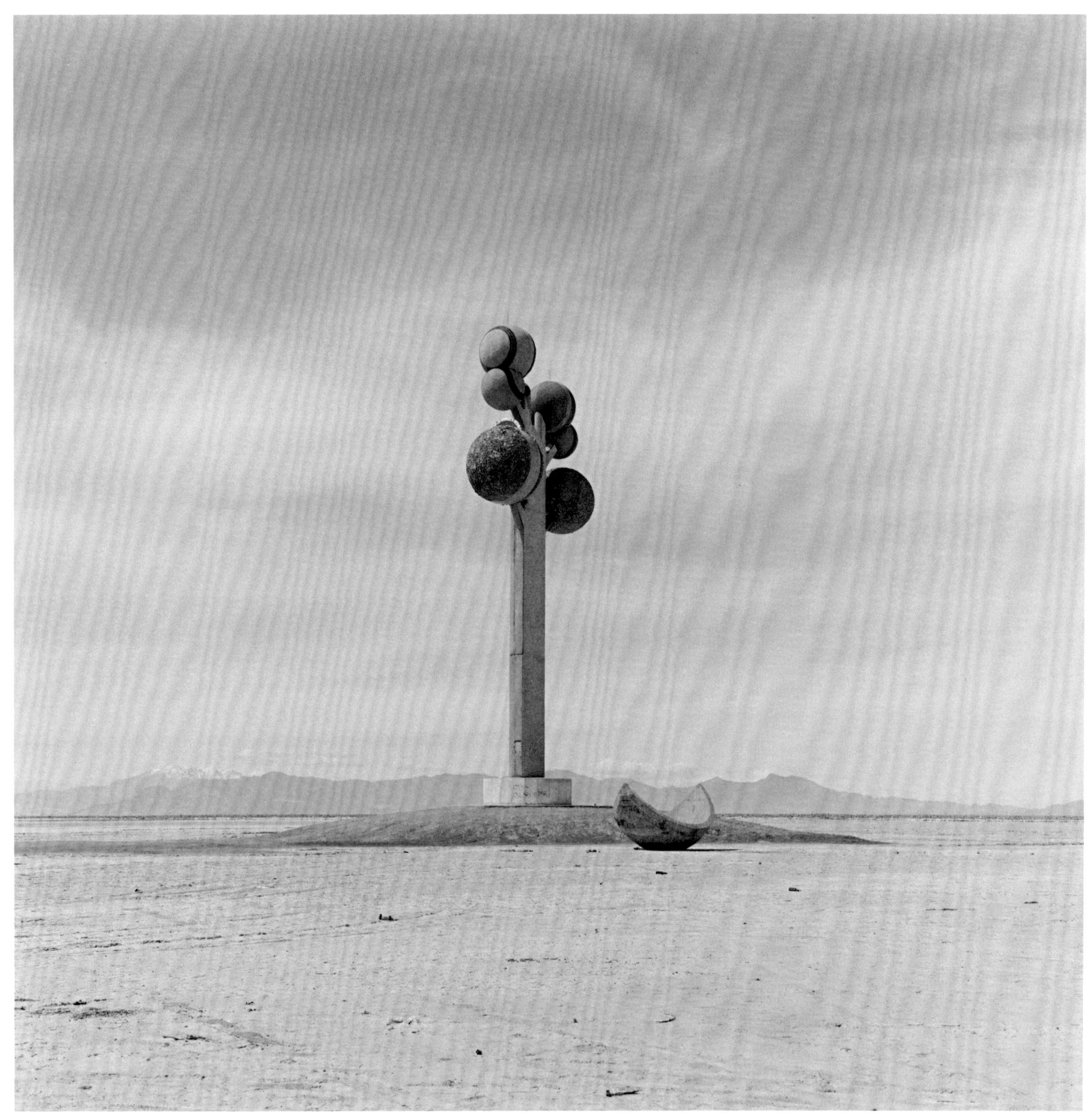

Near Wendover, Utah

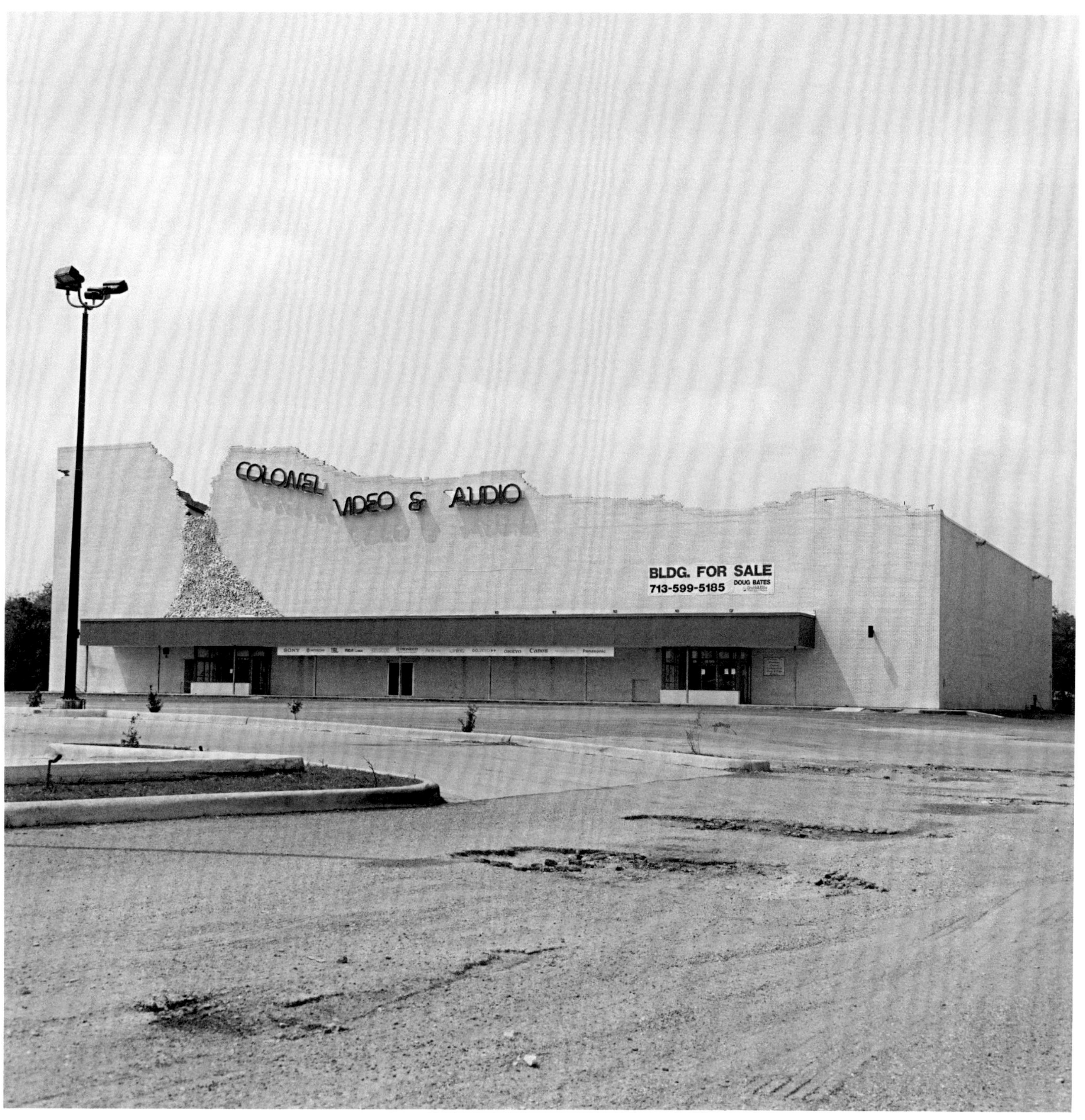

BEST Products Showroom
SITE with Maples-Jones Associates, 1975 • Houston, Texas

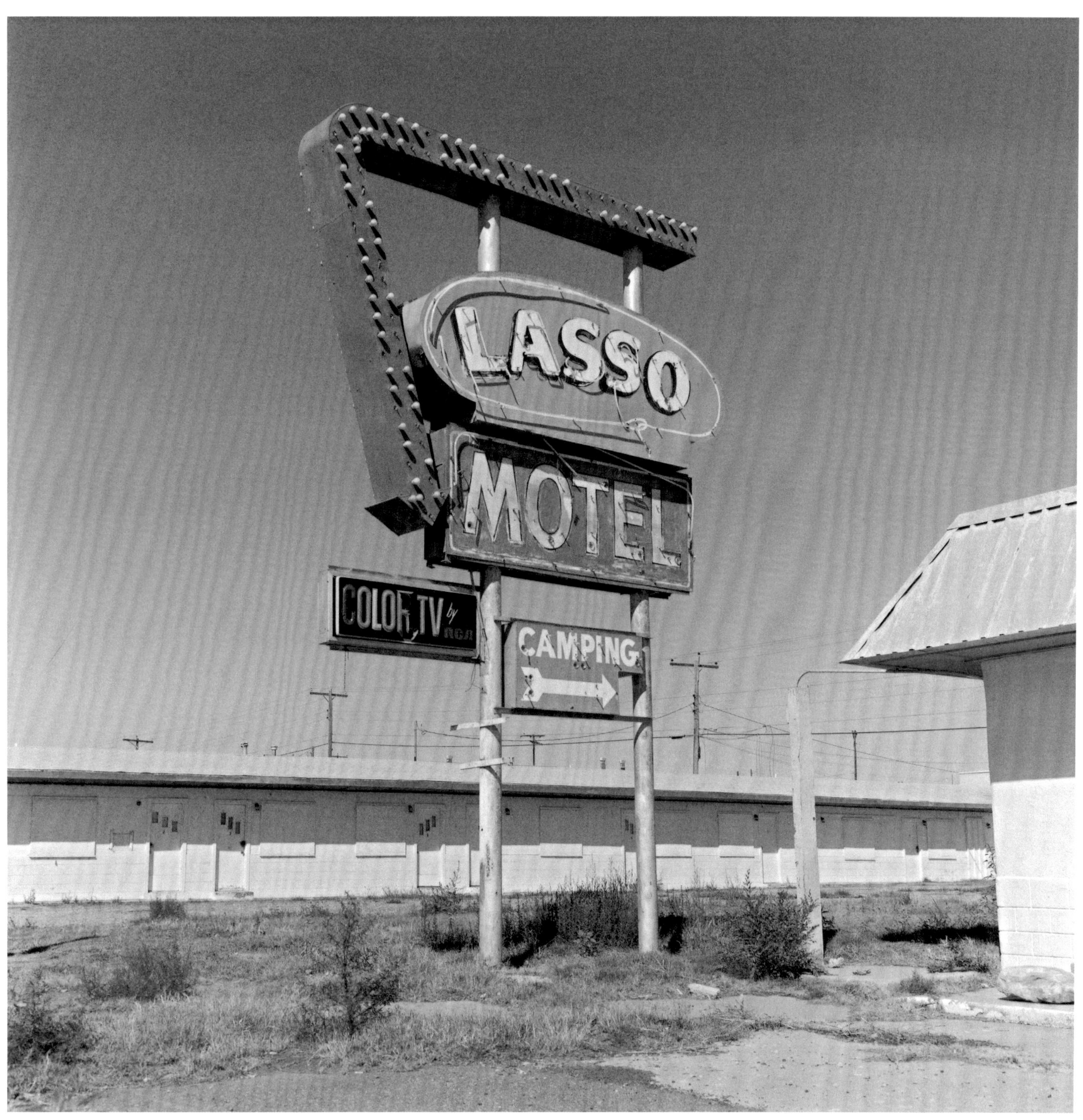

Lasso Motel
Tucumcari, New Mexico

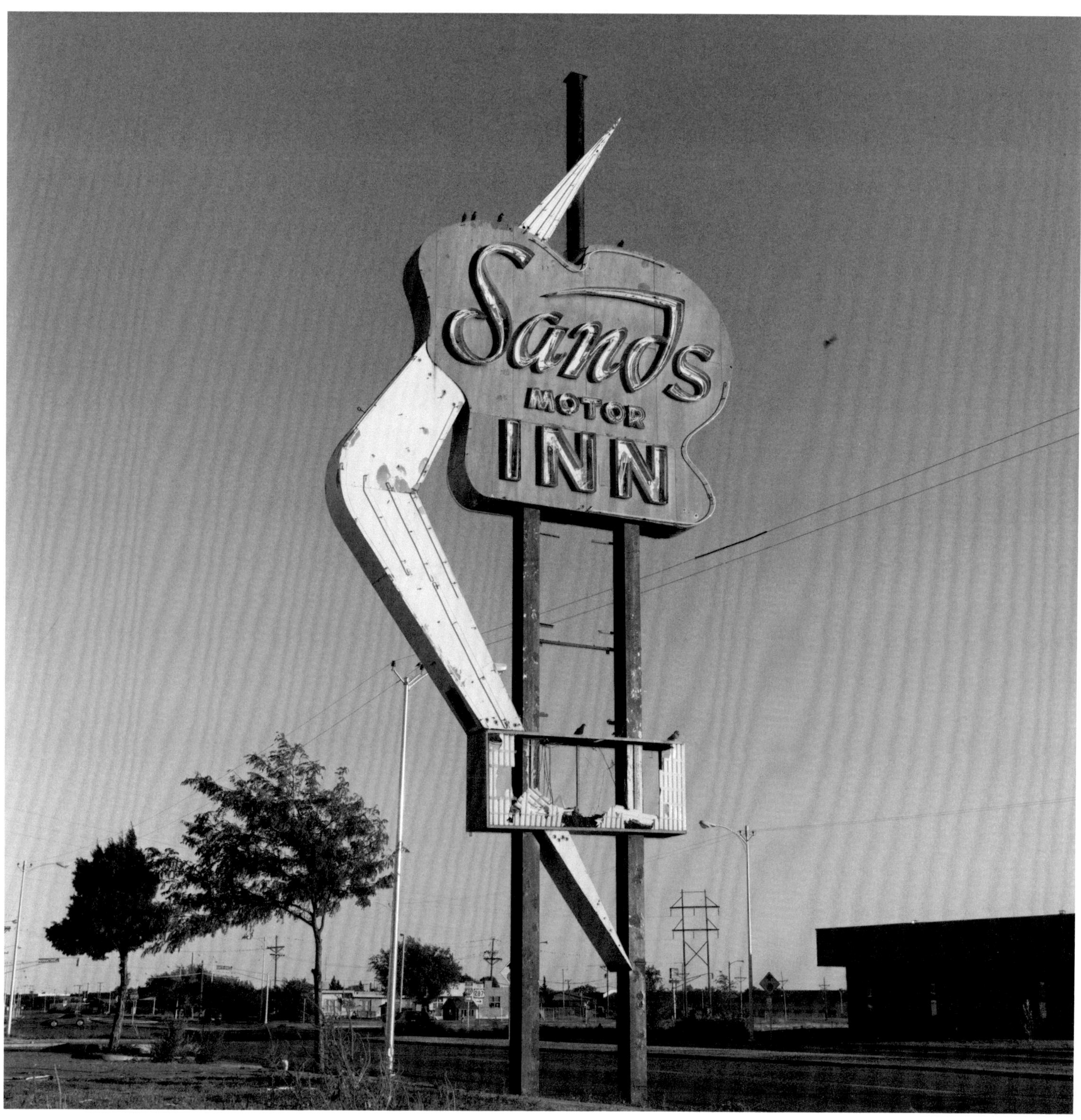

Sands Motor Inn
Amarillo, Texas

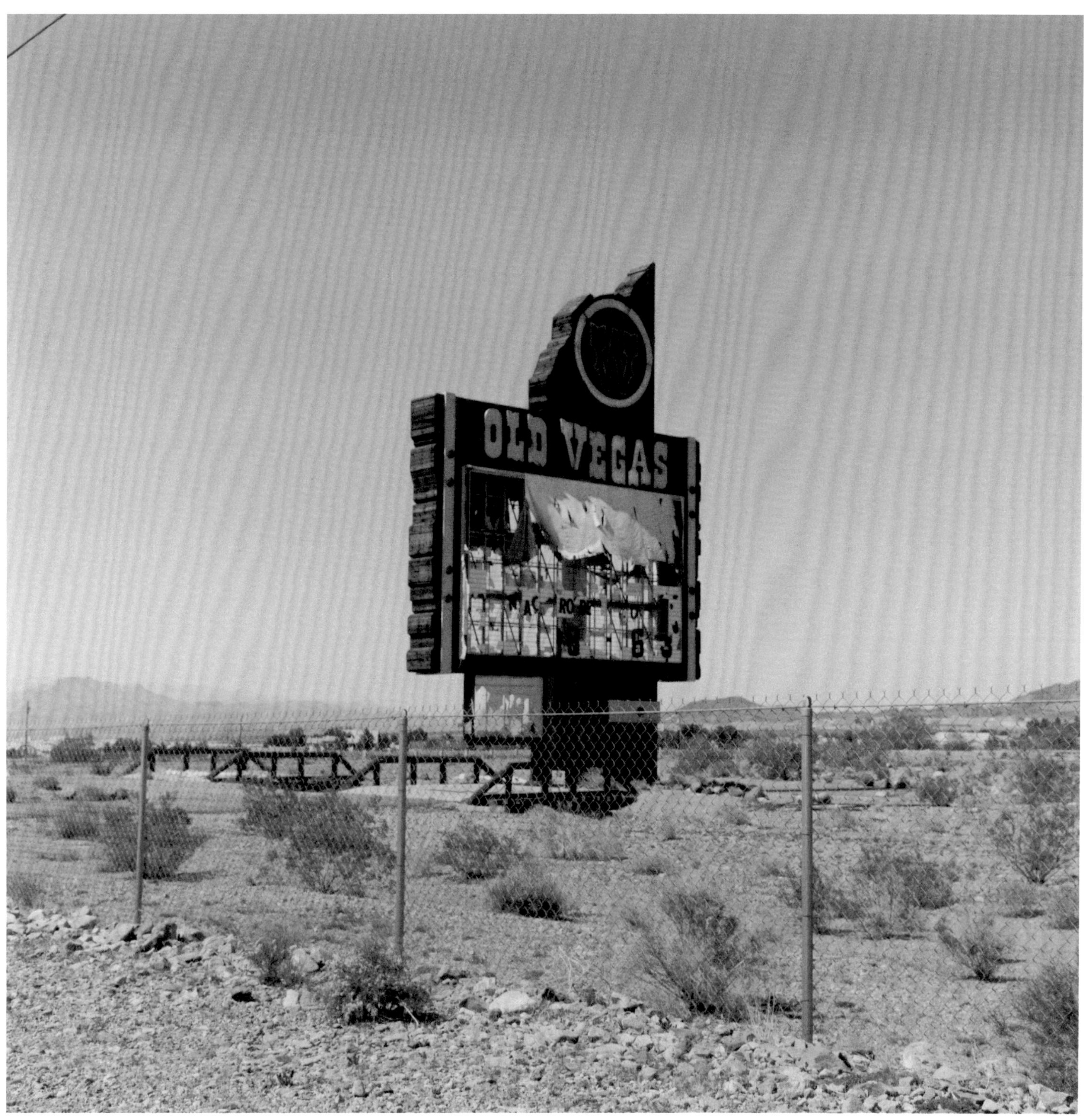

Old Vegas
Las Vegas, Nevada

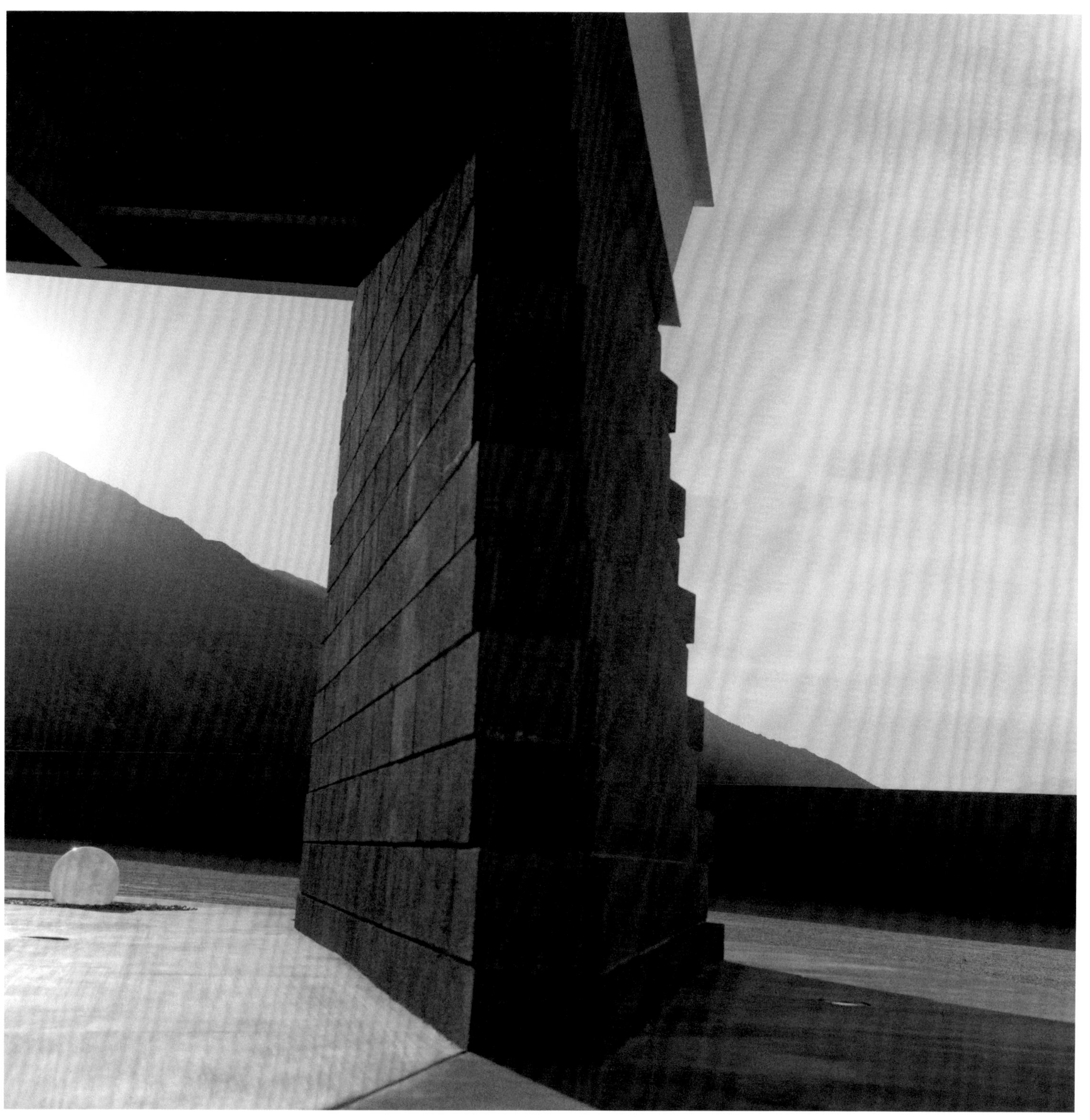

Gas Station
Albert Frey and Robson C. Chambers, 1965 • Palm Springs, California

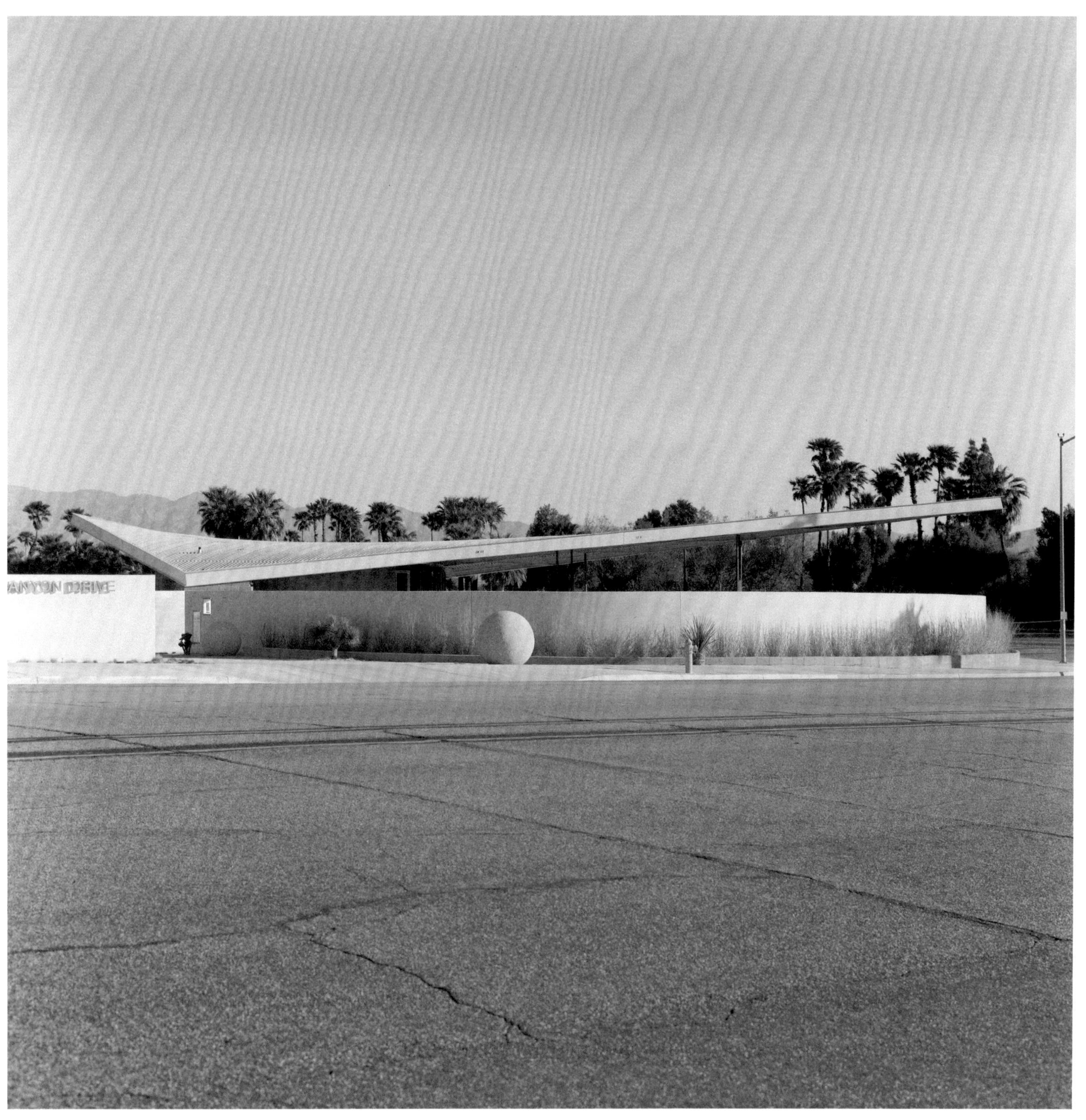

Gas Station
Albert Frey and Robson C. Chambers, 1965 • Palm Springs, California

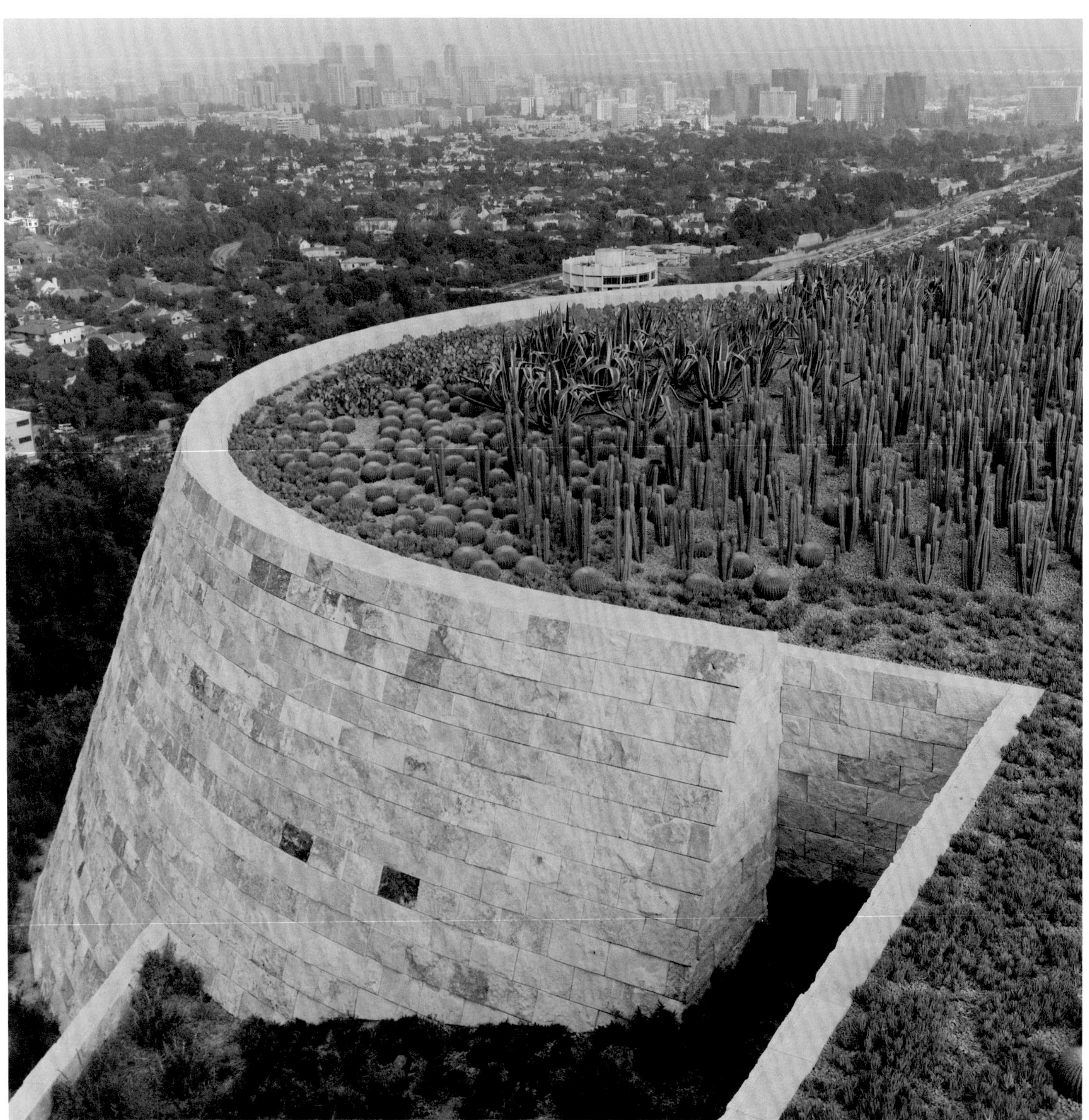

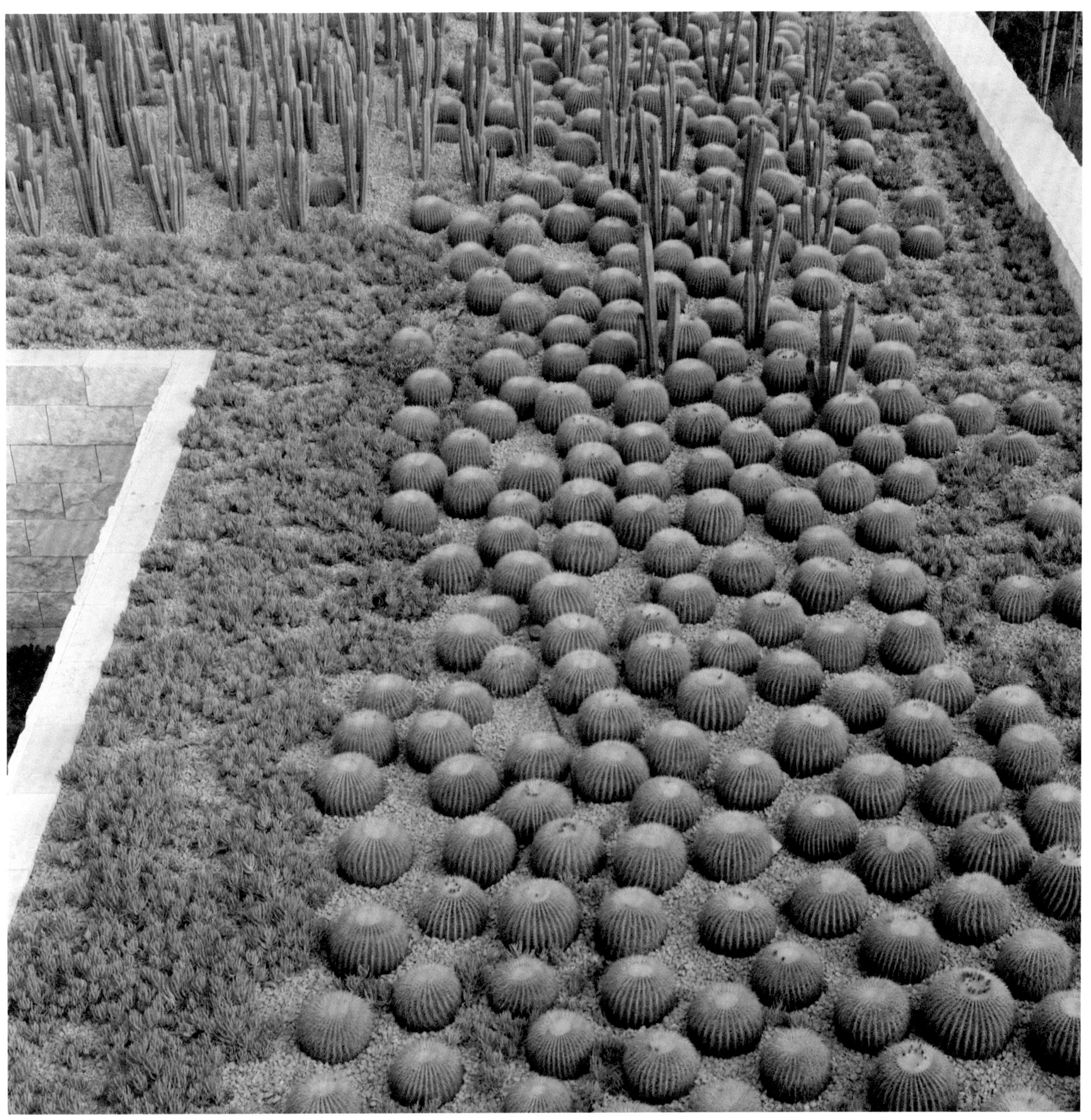

Getty Center
Richard Meier & Partners, 1984–97 · Brentwood, California

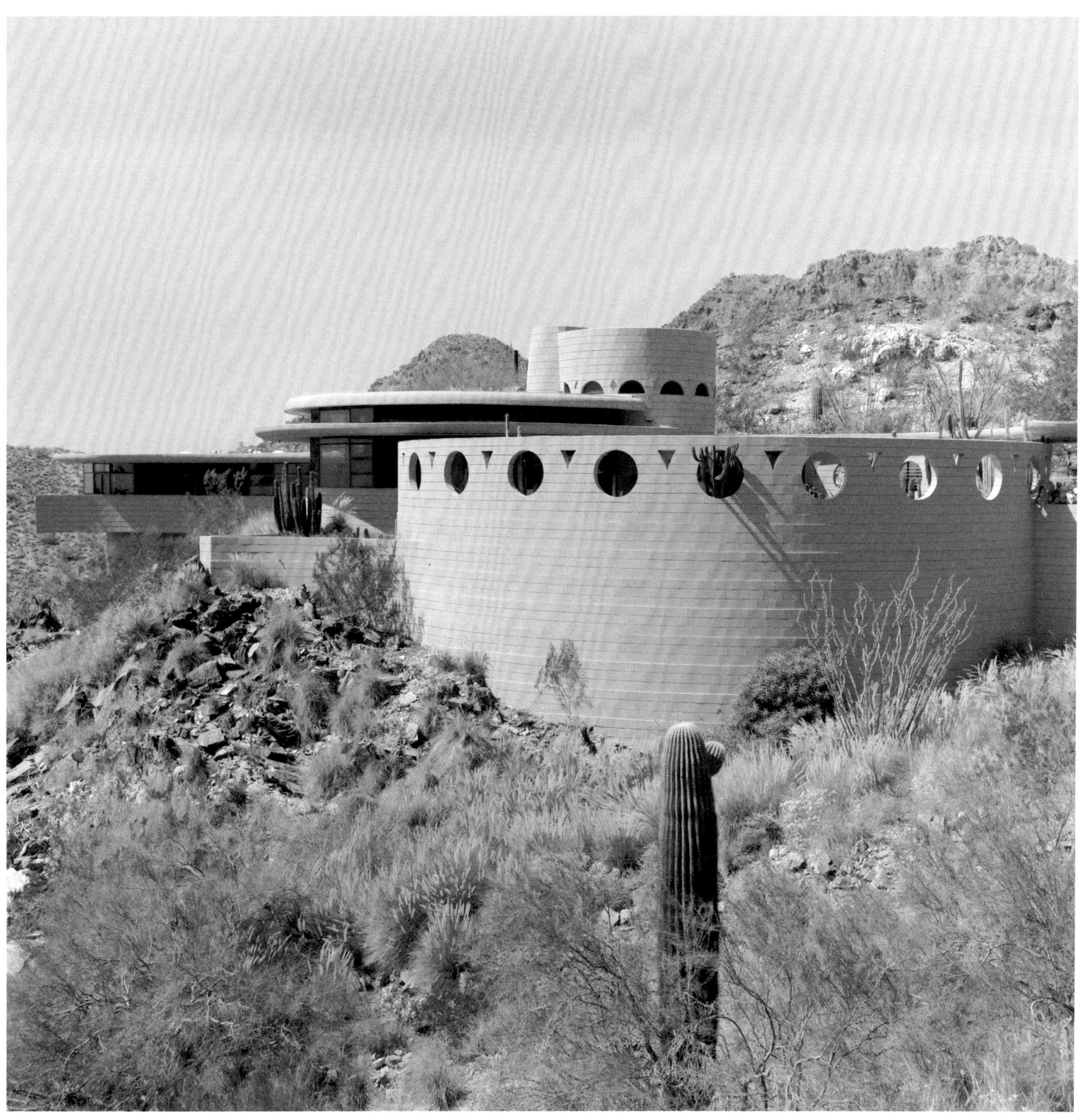

Residence
Frank Lloyd Wright • Phoenix, Arizona

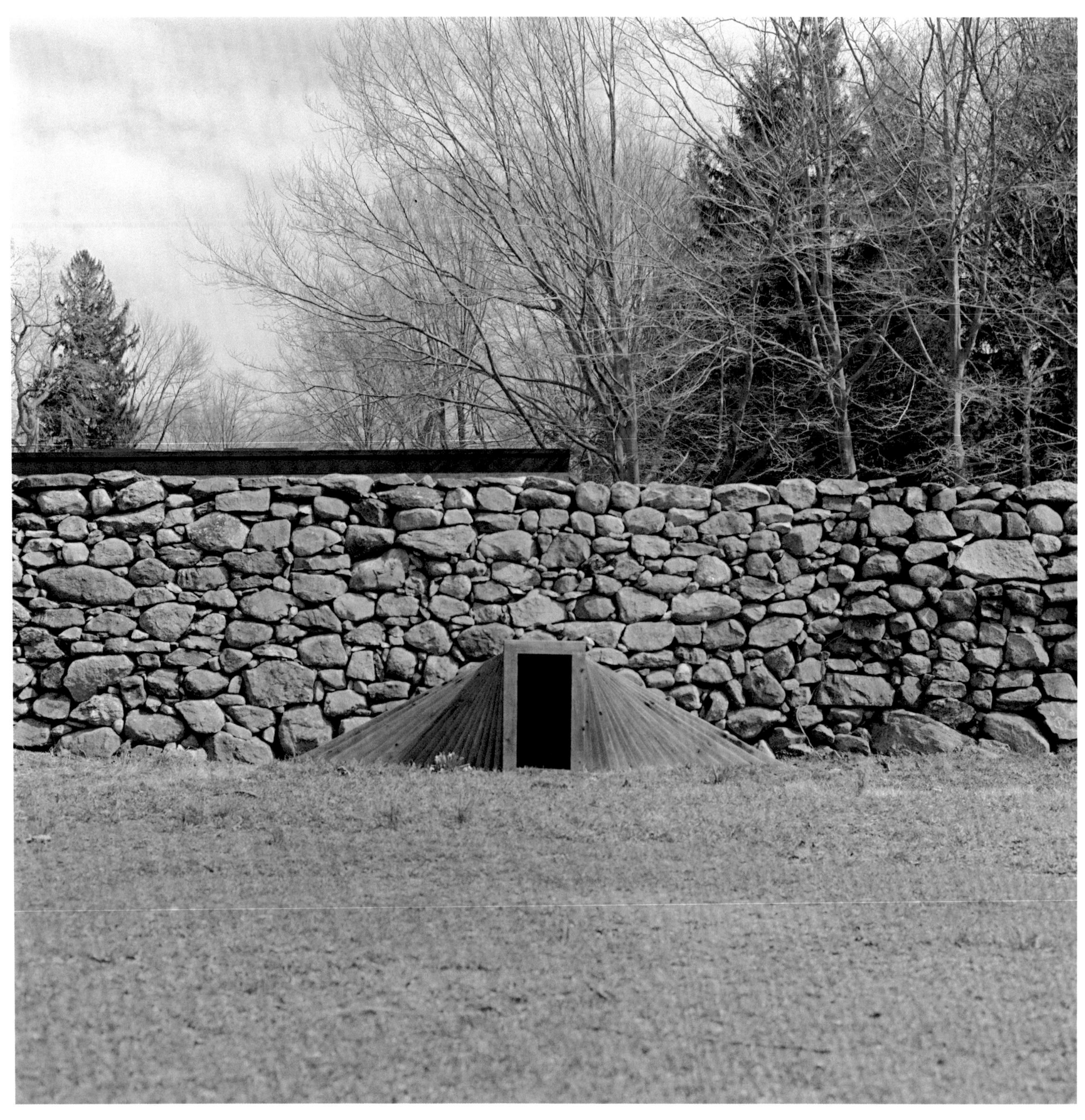

Doghouse
Philip Johnson, 1996 • New Canaan, Connecticut

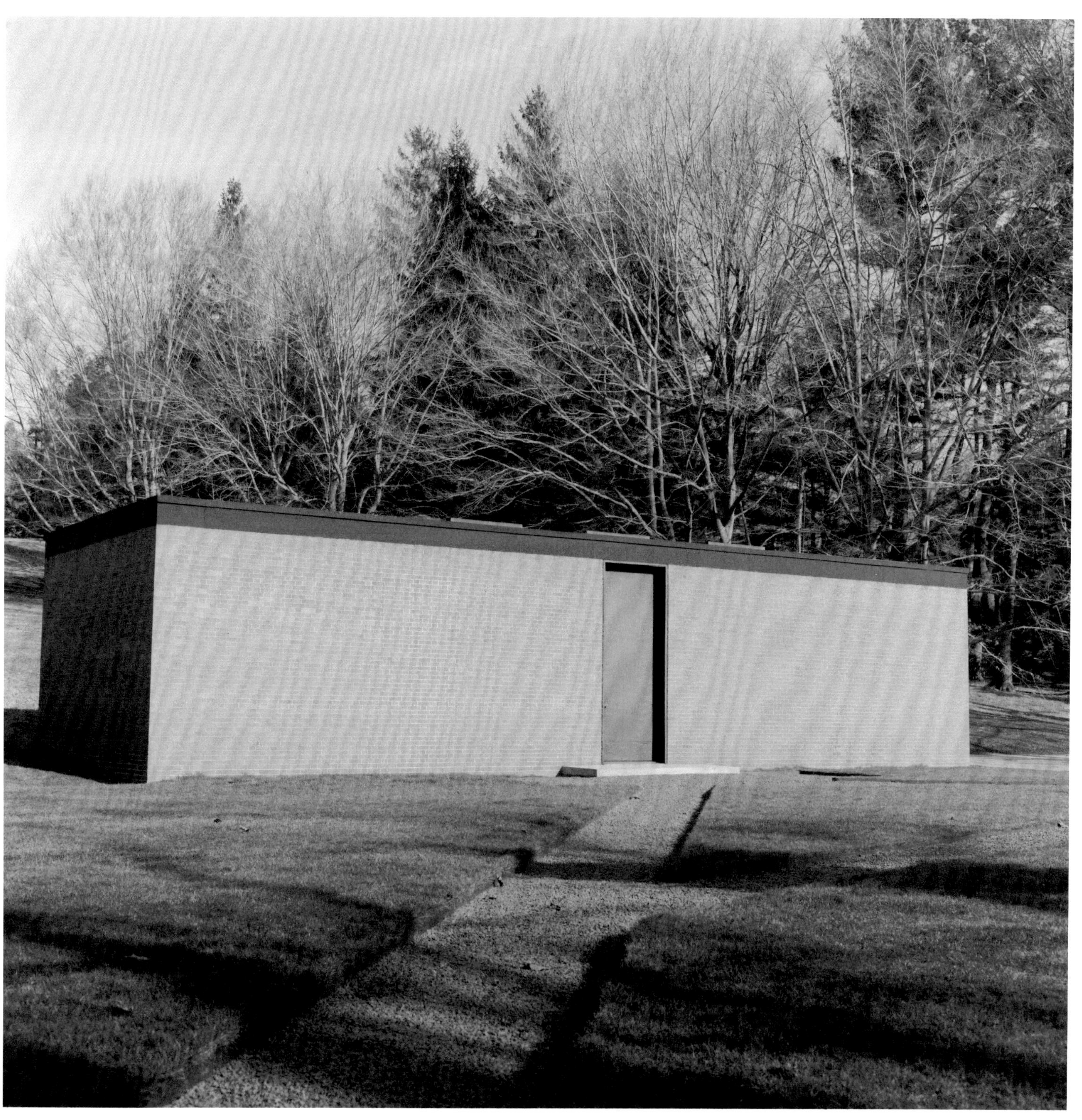

Brick House
Philip Johnson, 1953 • New Canaan, Connecticut

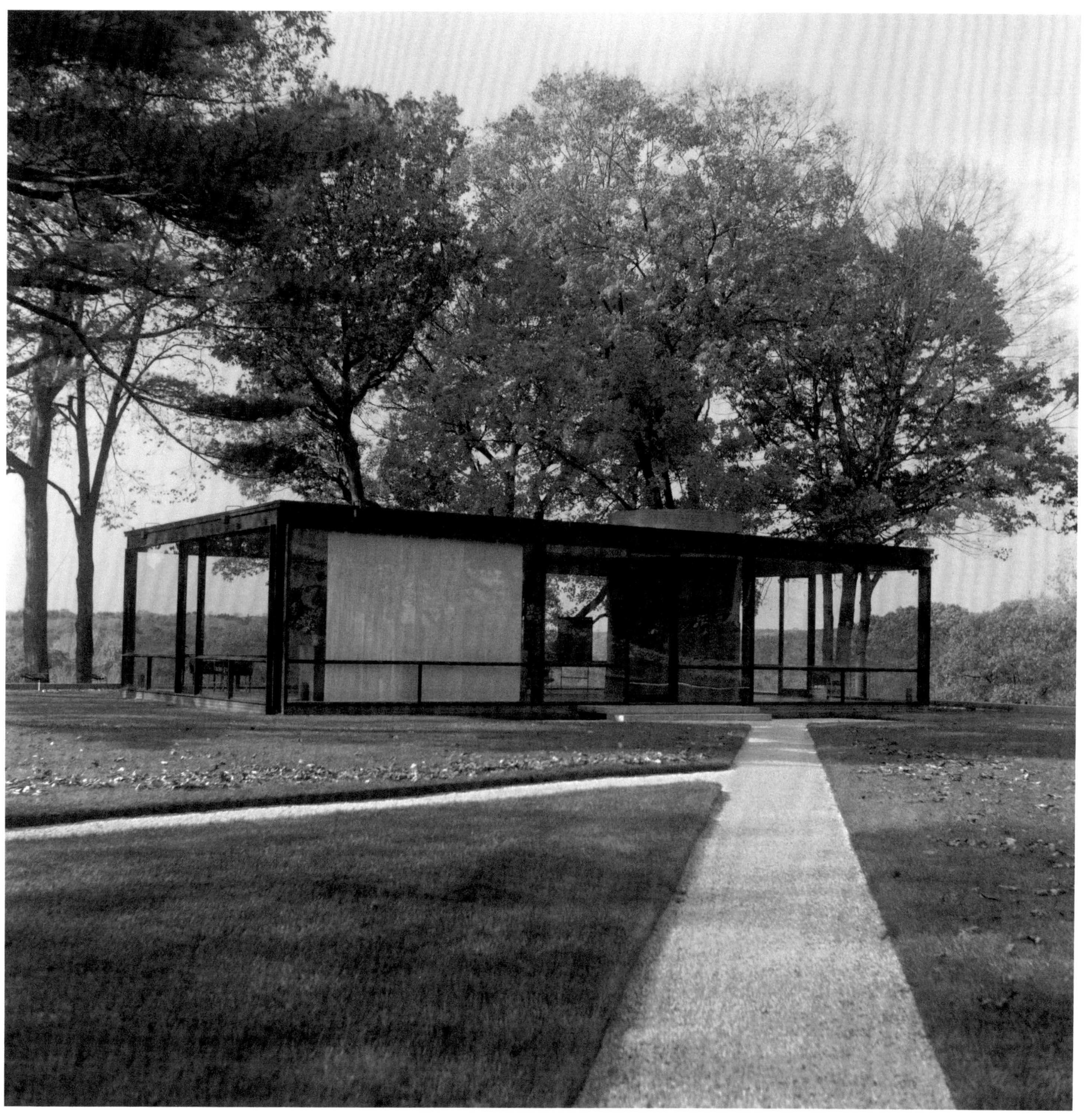

Glass House
Philip Johnson, 1949 · New Canaan, Connecticut

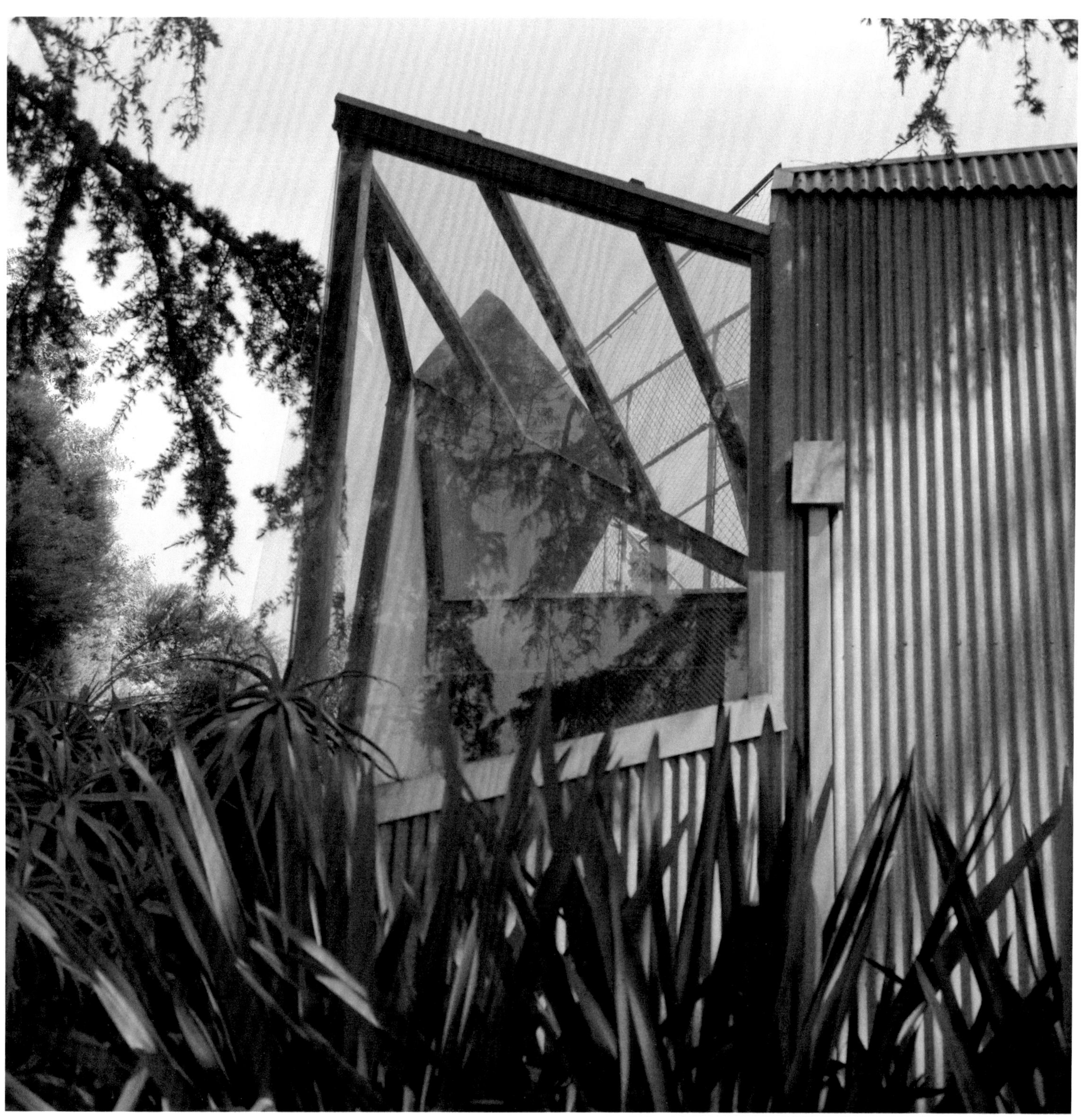

Gehry Residence
Frank O. Gehry, 1977– • Santa Monica, California

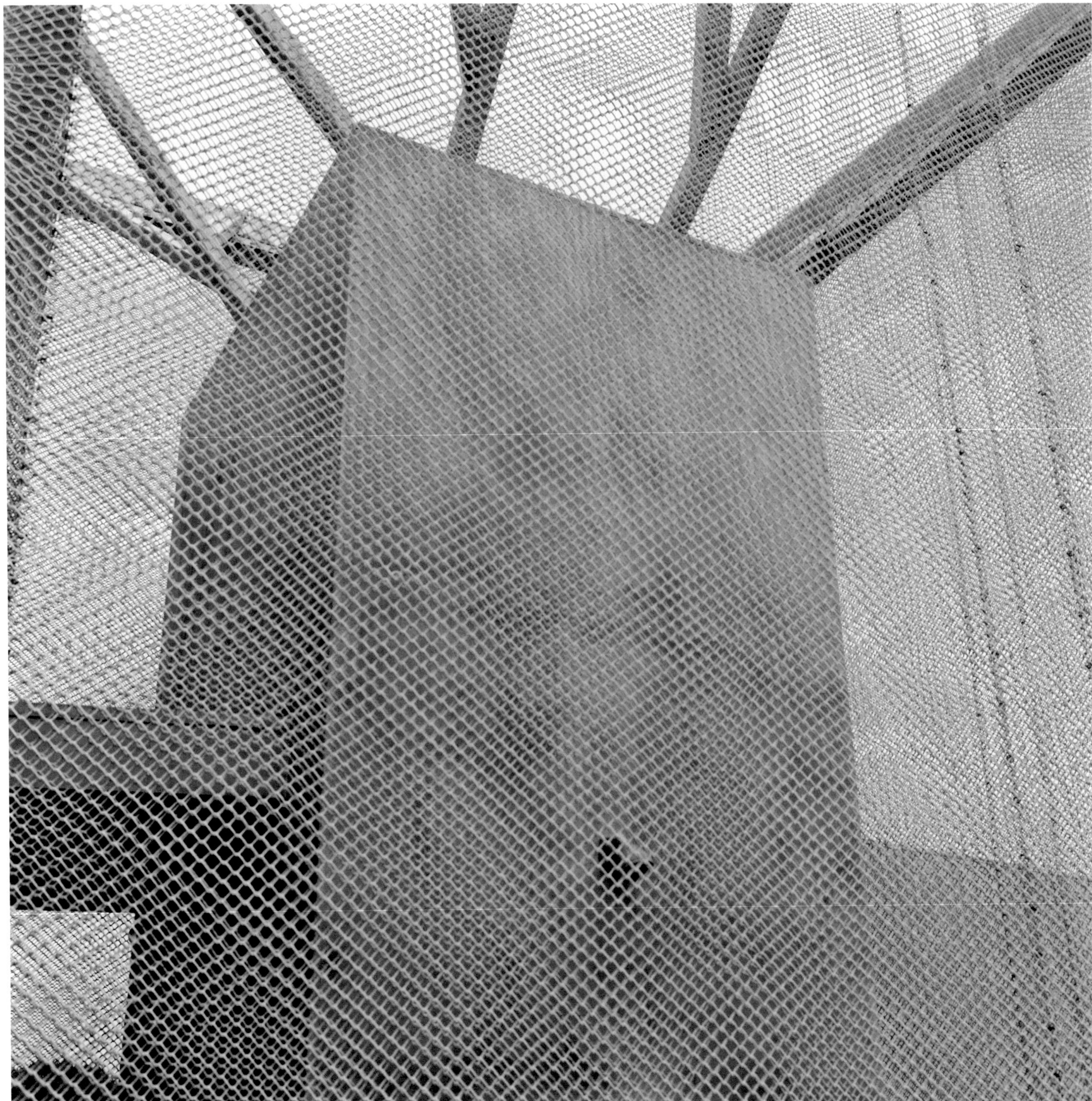

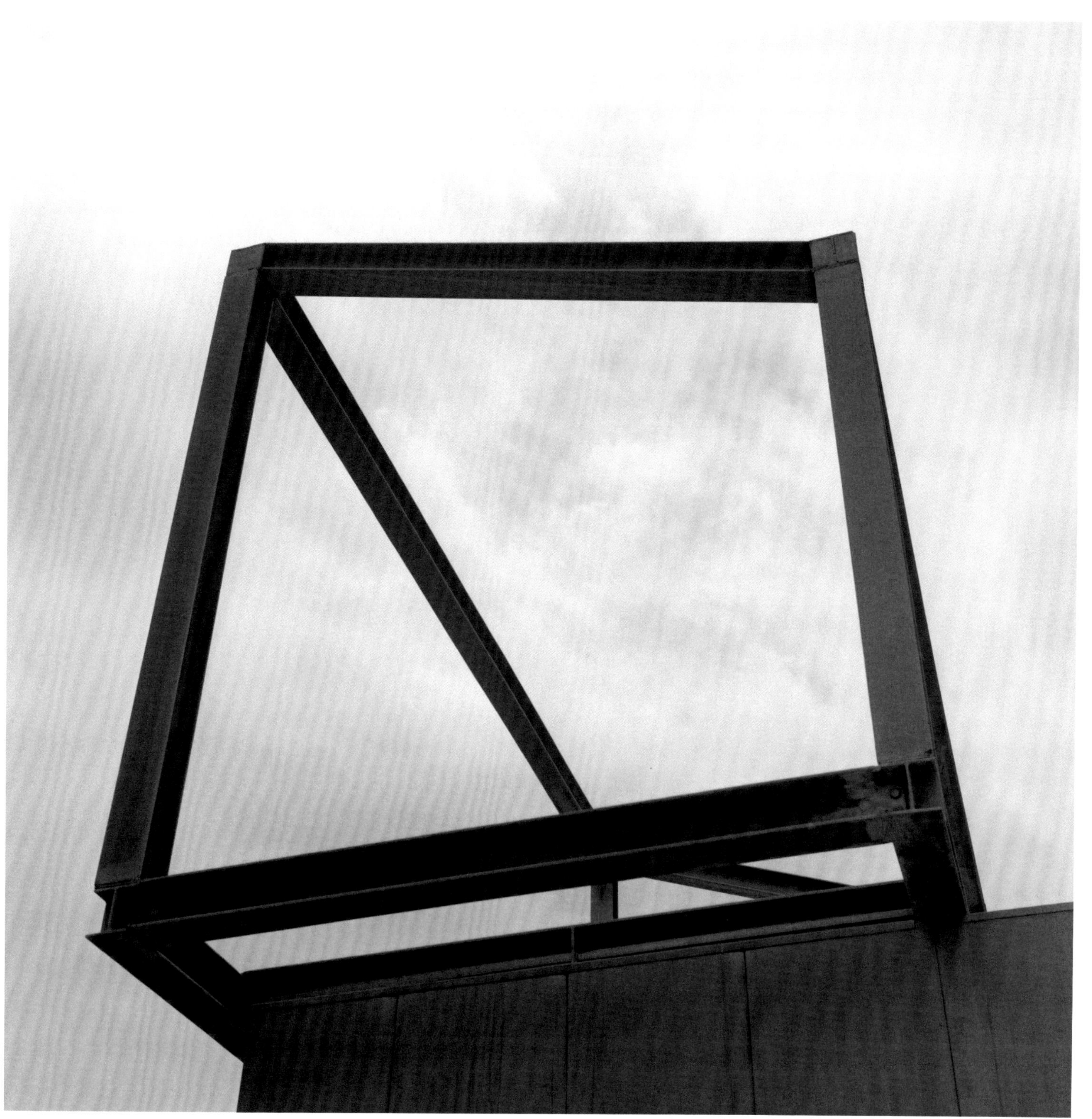

Edgemar
Frank O. Gehry, 1984–88 • Santa Monica, California

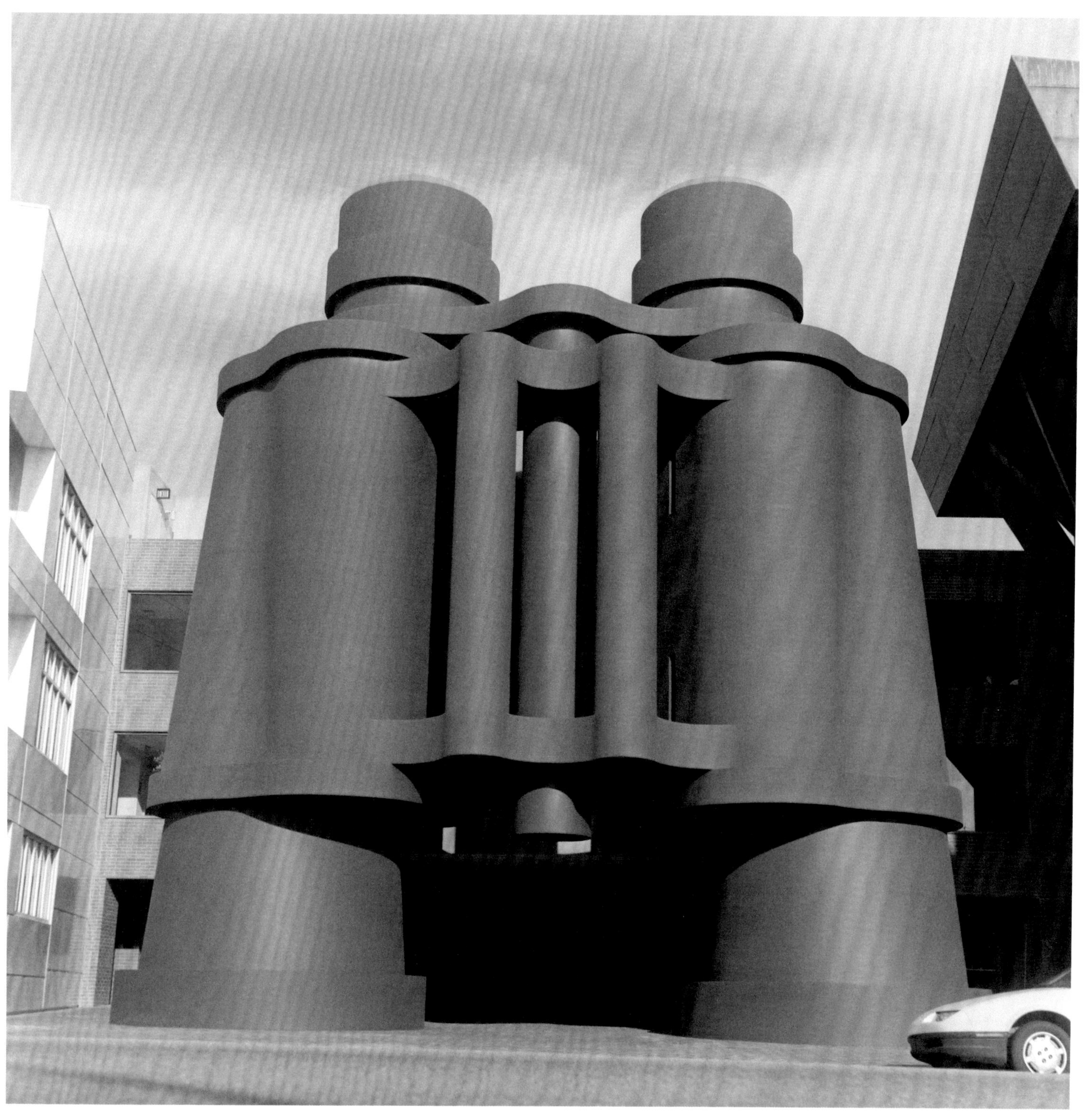

Chiat/Day Building
Frank O. Gehry and Associates with Claes Oldenburg and Coosje van Bruggen, 1985–91
Venice, California

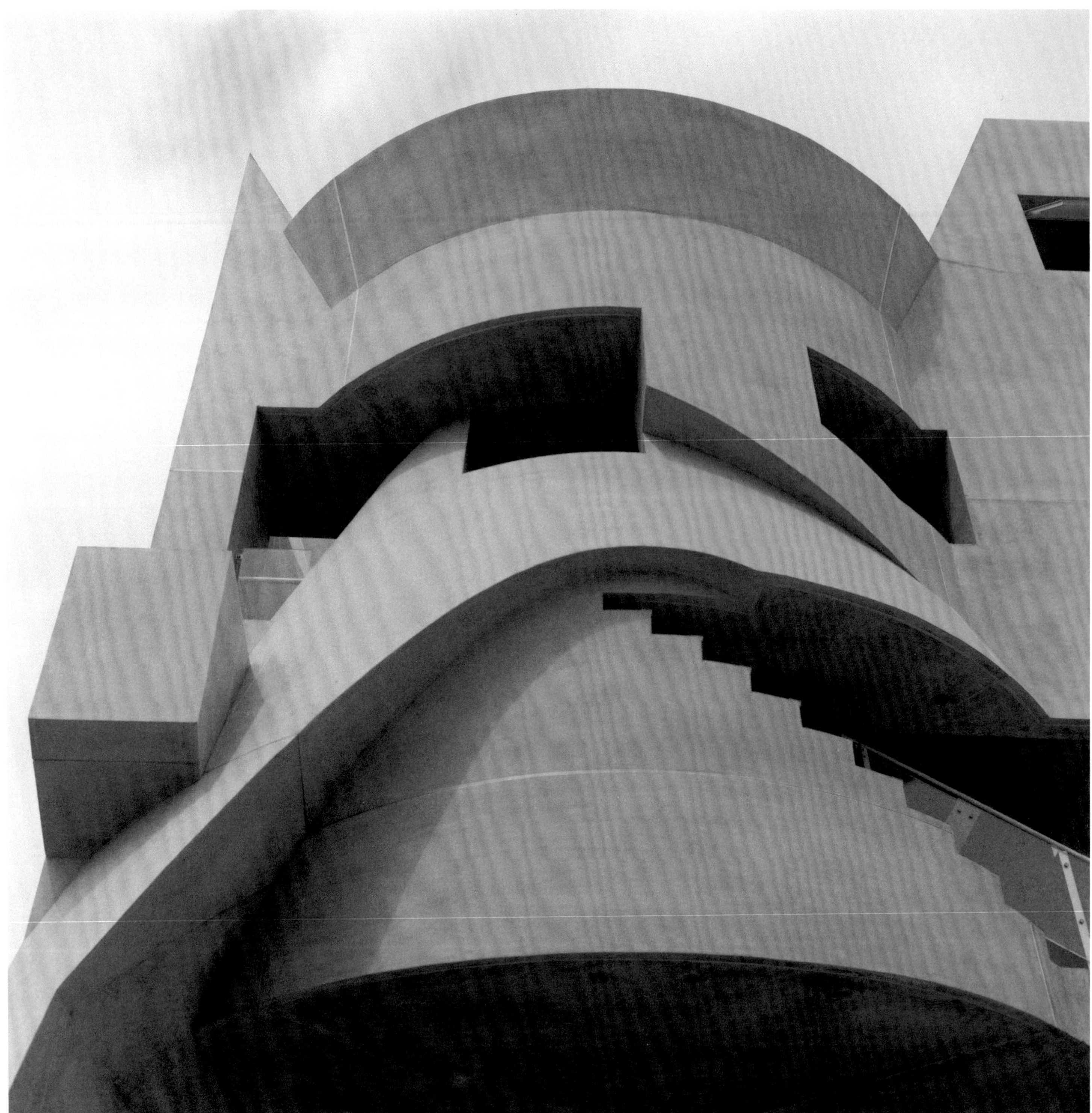

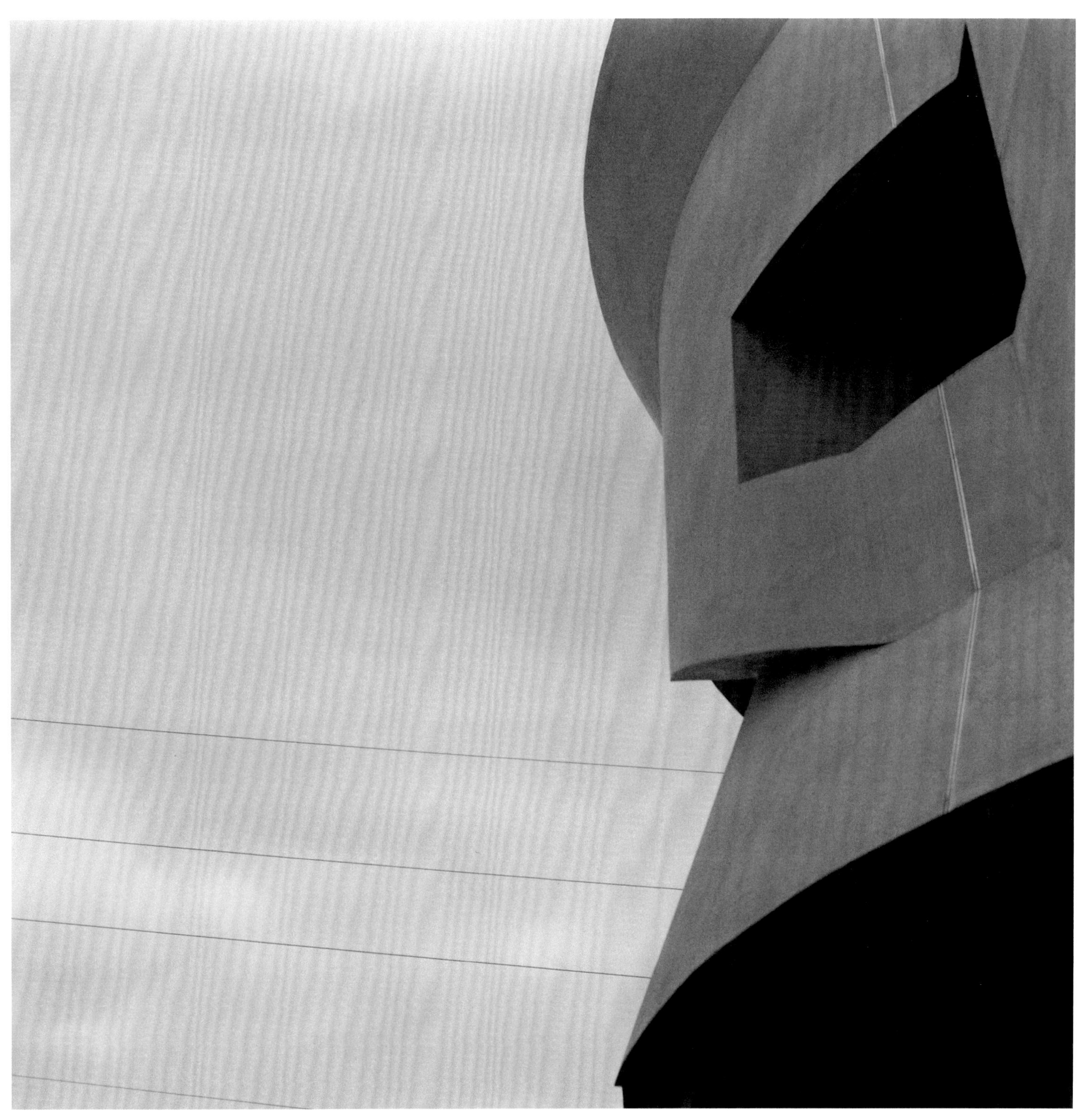

Samitaur, Kodak Complex
Eric Owen Moss, 1996 • Culver City, California

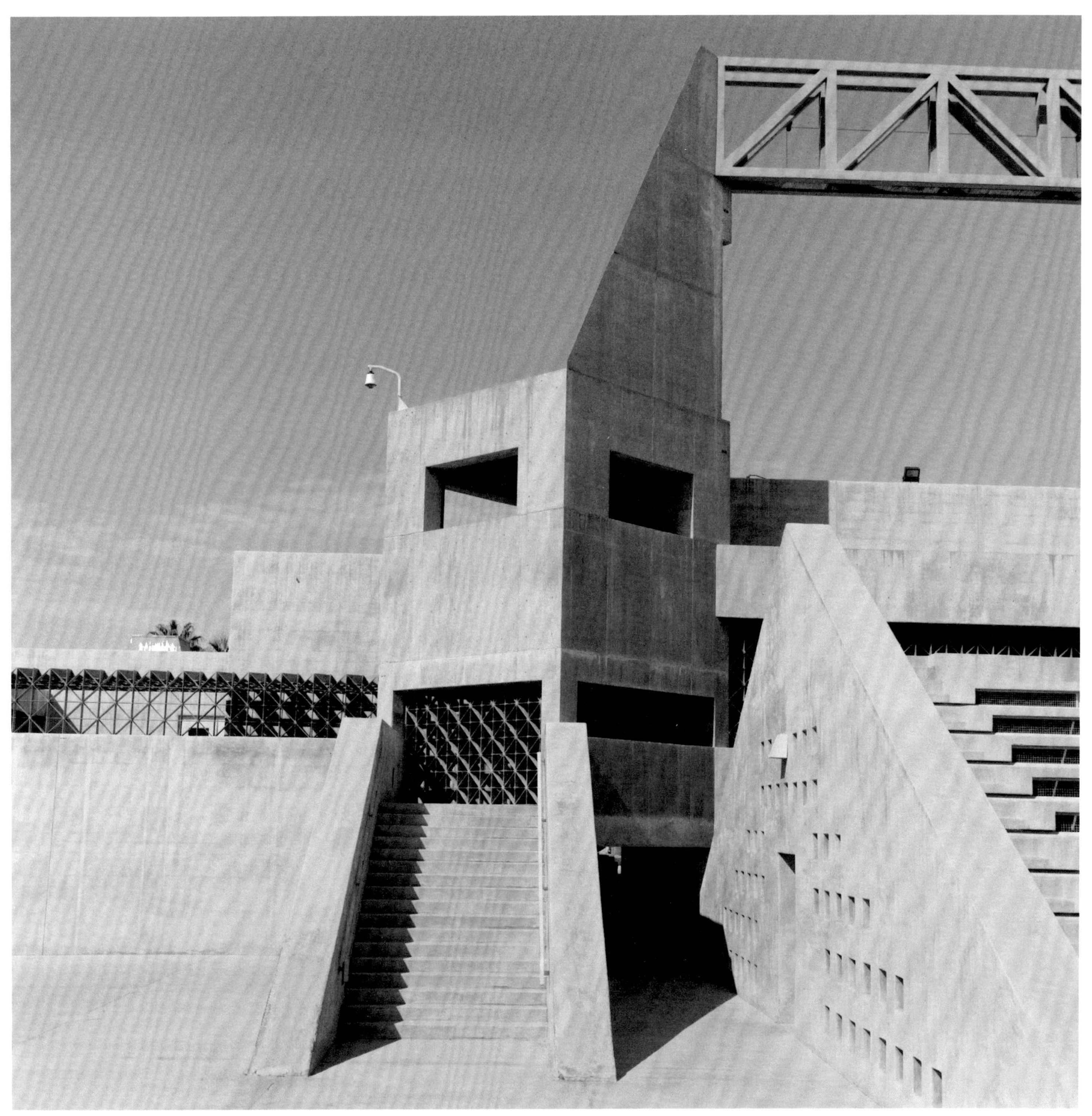

Nelson Fine Arts Center, Arizona State University
Antoine Predock, 1985–89 • Tempe, Arizona

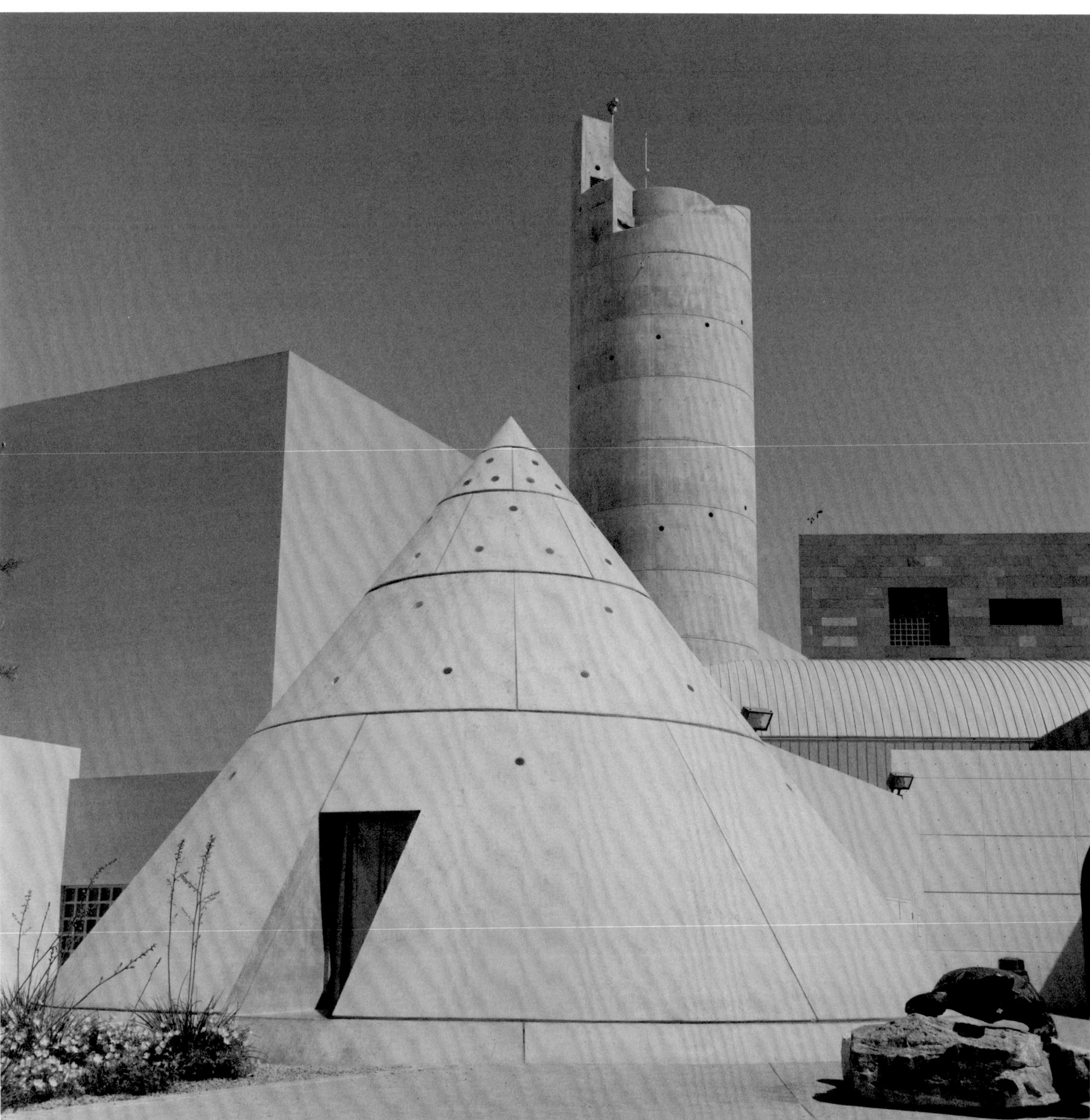

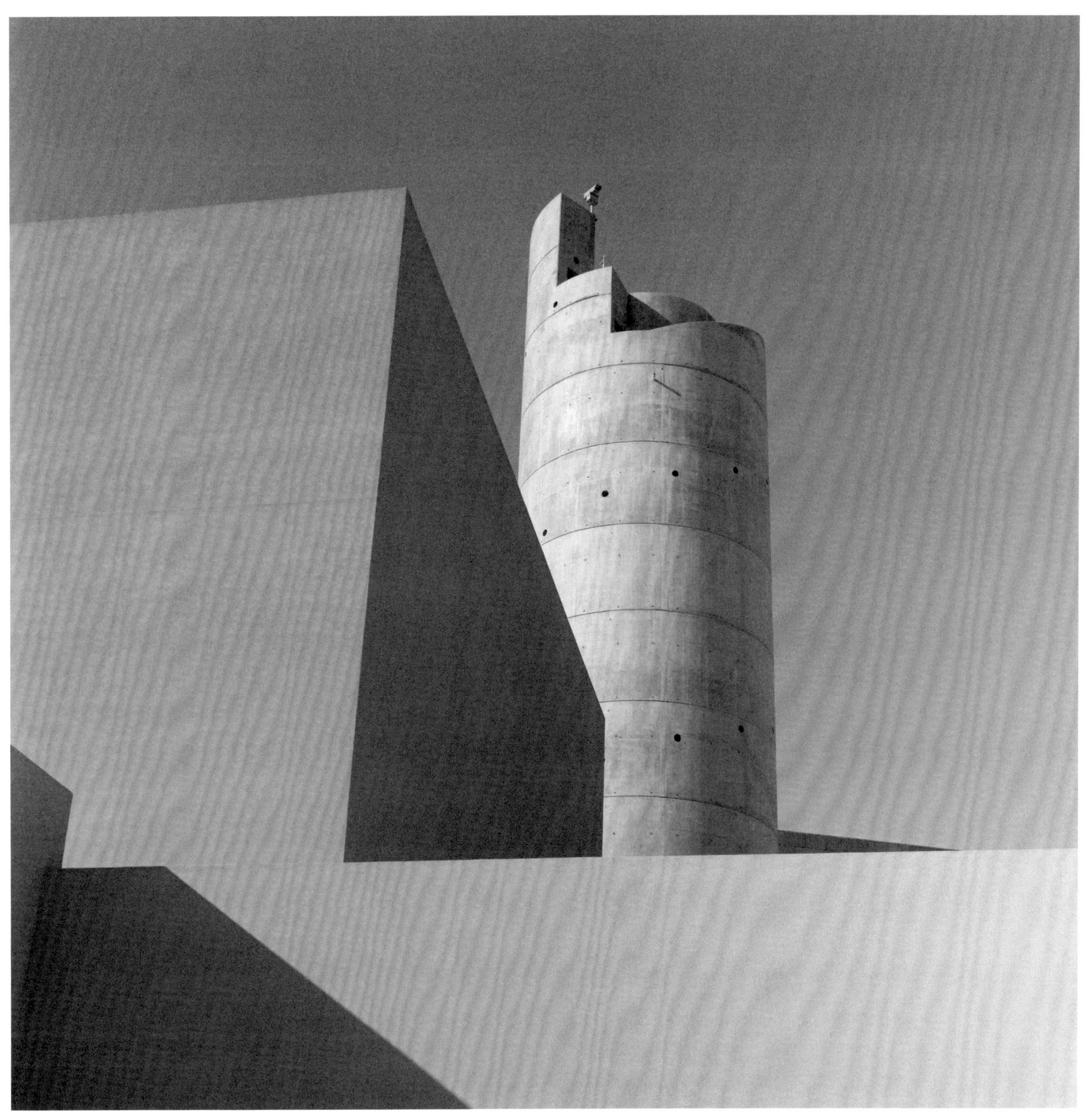

Las Vegas Library and Children's Museum
Antoine Predock, 1990 • Las Vegas, Nevada

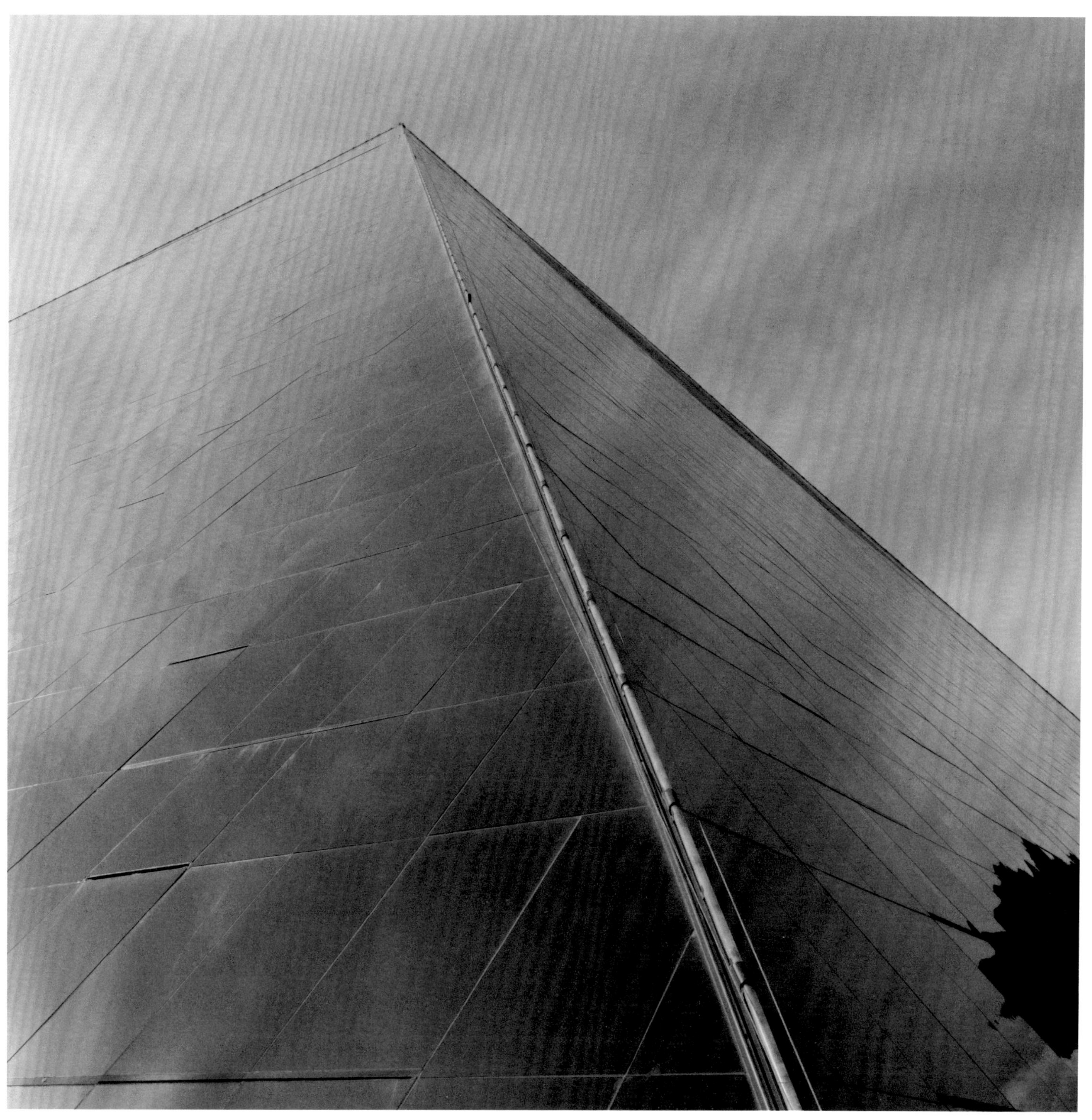

Luxor
Veldon Simpson, 1993 • Las Vegas, Nevada

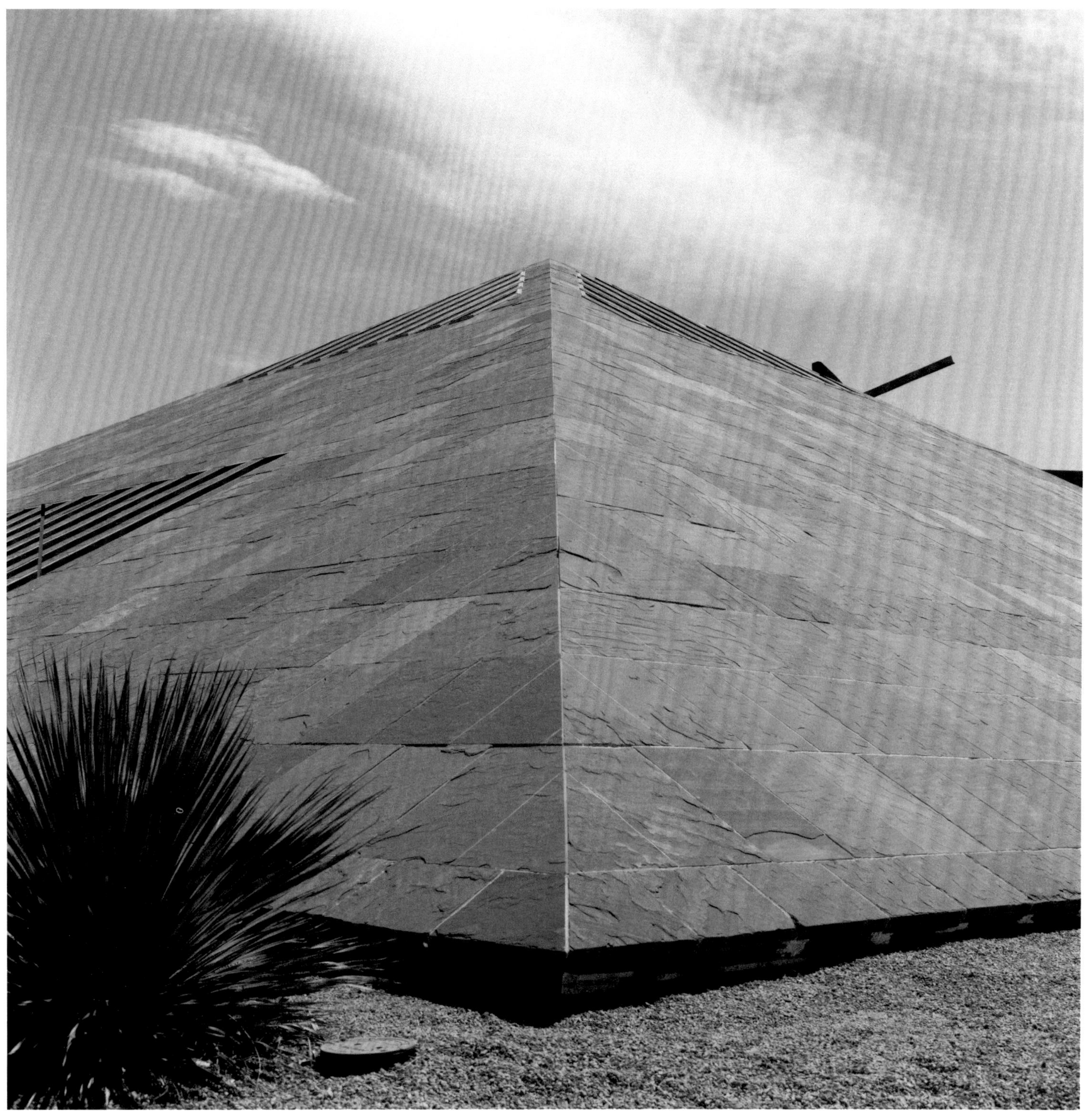

Pyramid
Las Vegas, Nevada

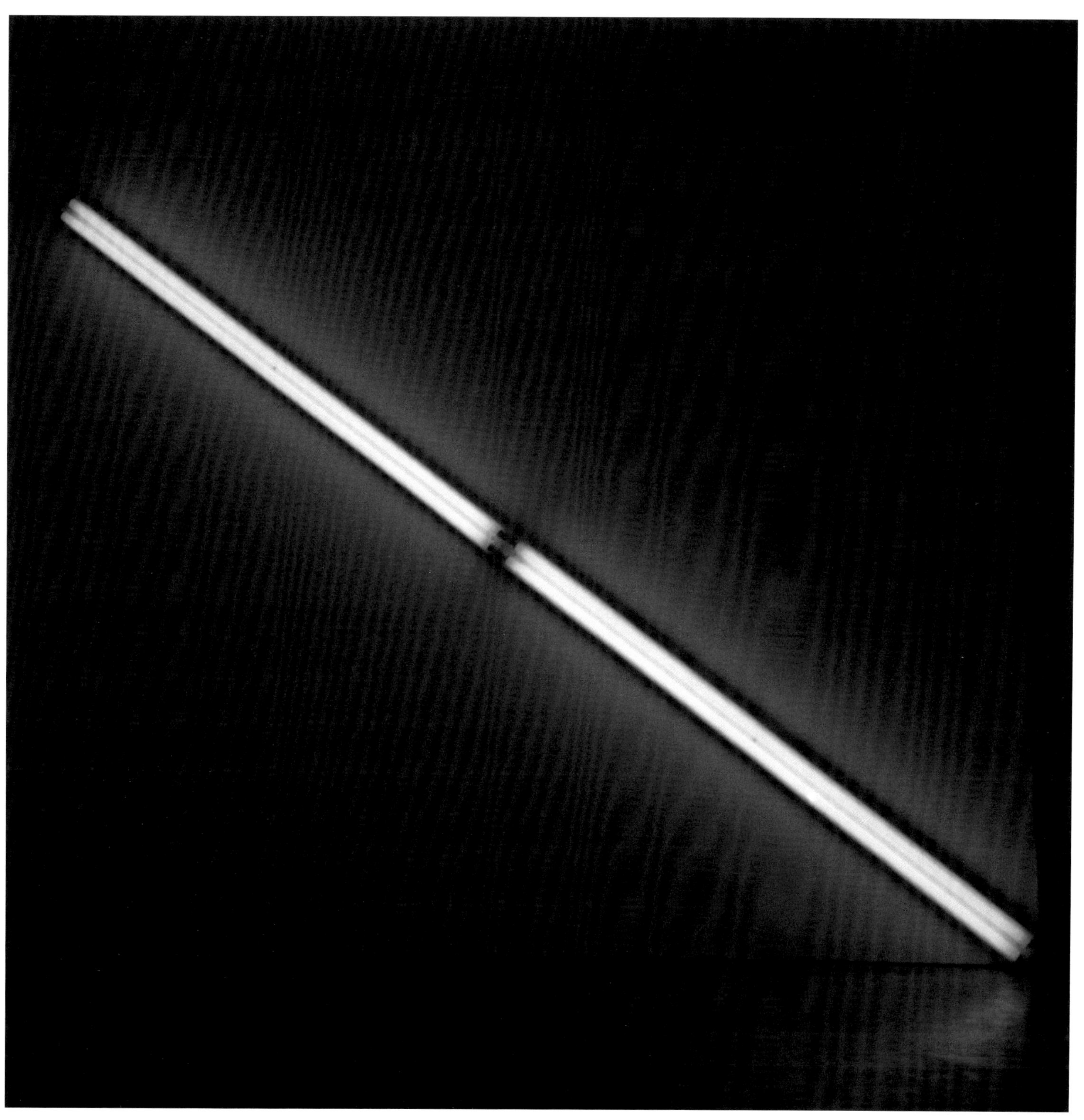

Untitled, Installation for Richmond Hall, Menil Collection
Dan Flavin, 1996 • Houston, Texas

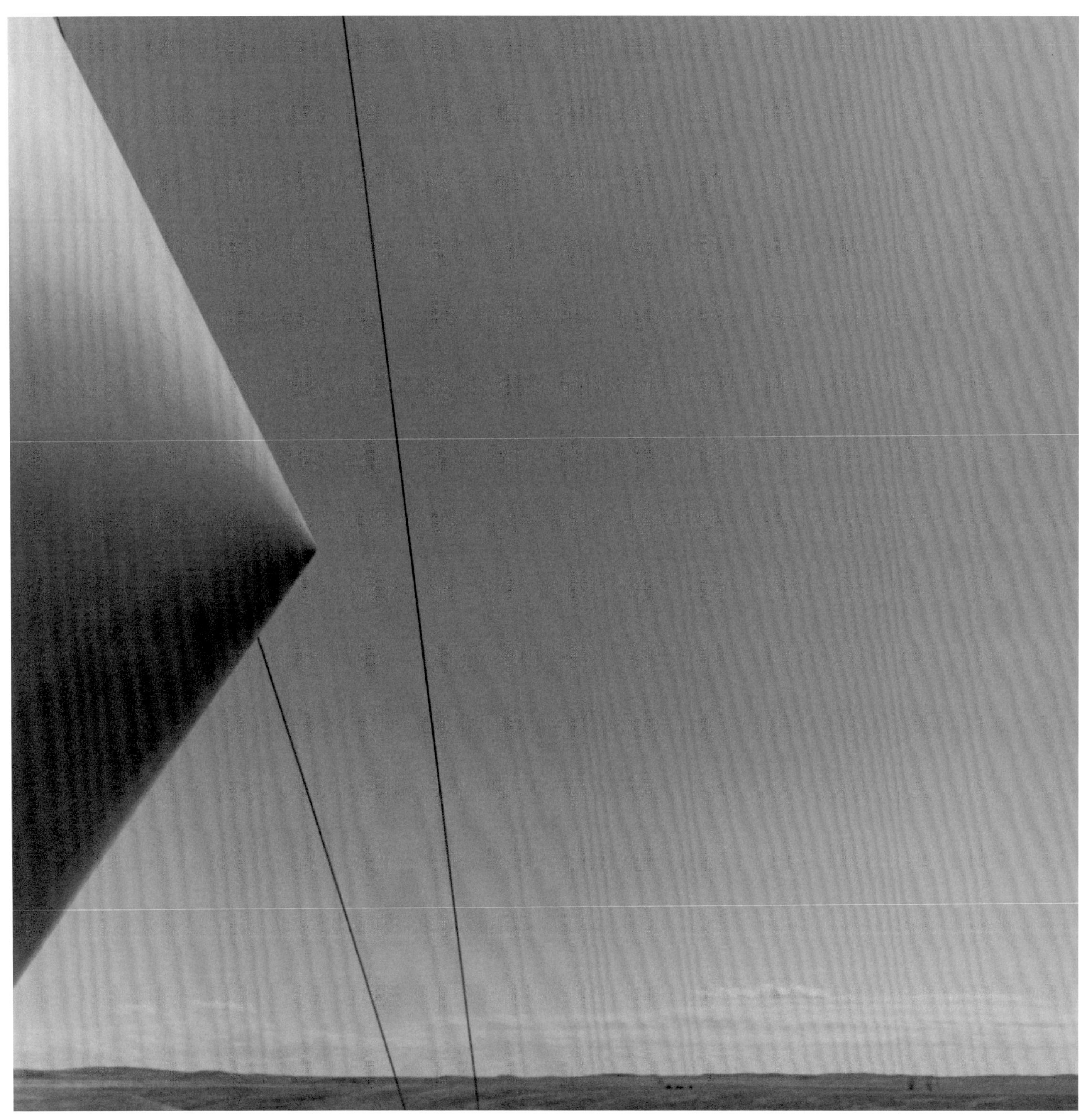

Telecommunications Tower
Badlands, South Dakota

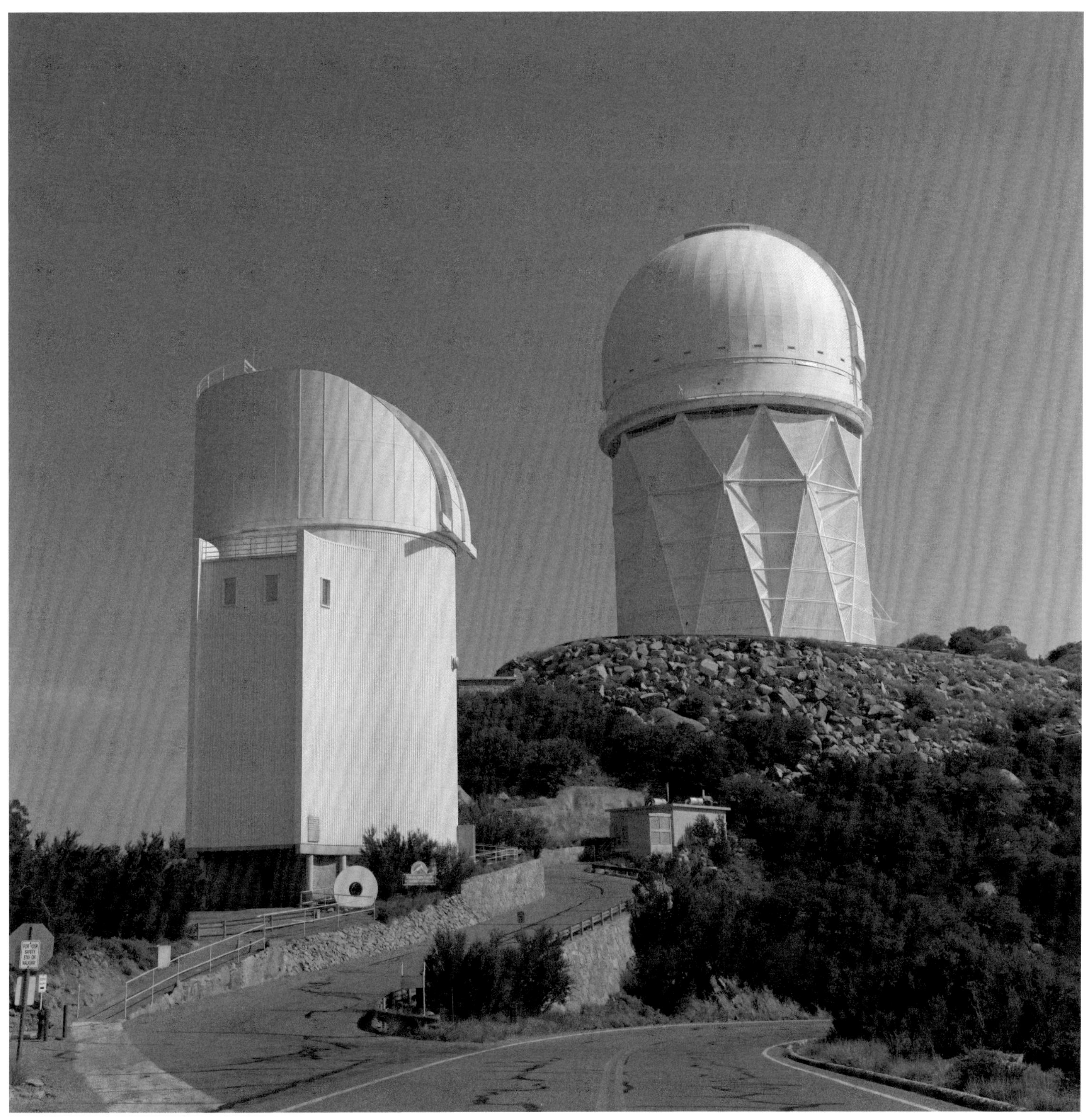

National Observatory
1960 • *Kitt Peak, Arizona*

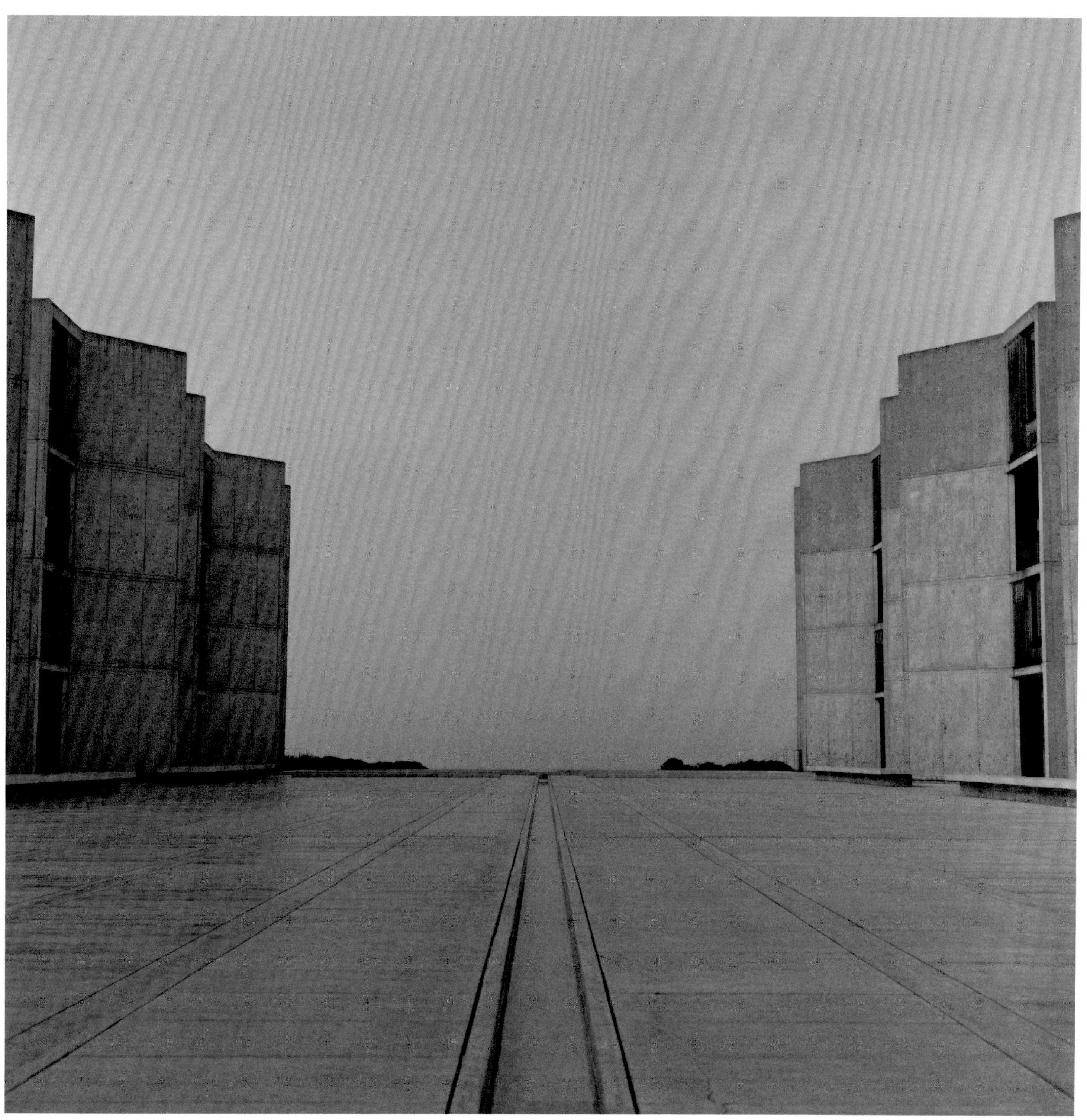

Jonas Salk Institute for Biological Studies
Louis I. Kahn, 1959–65 • La Jolla, California

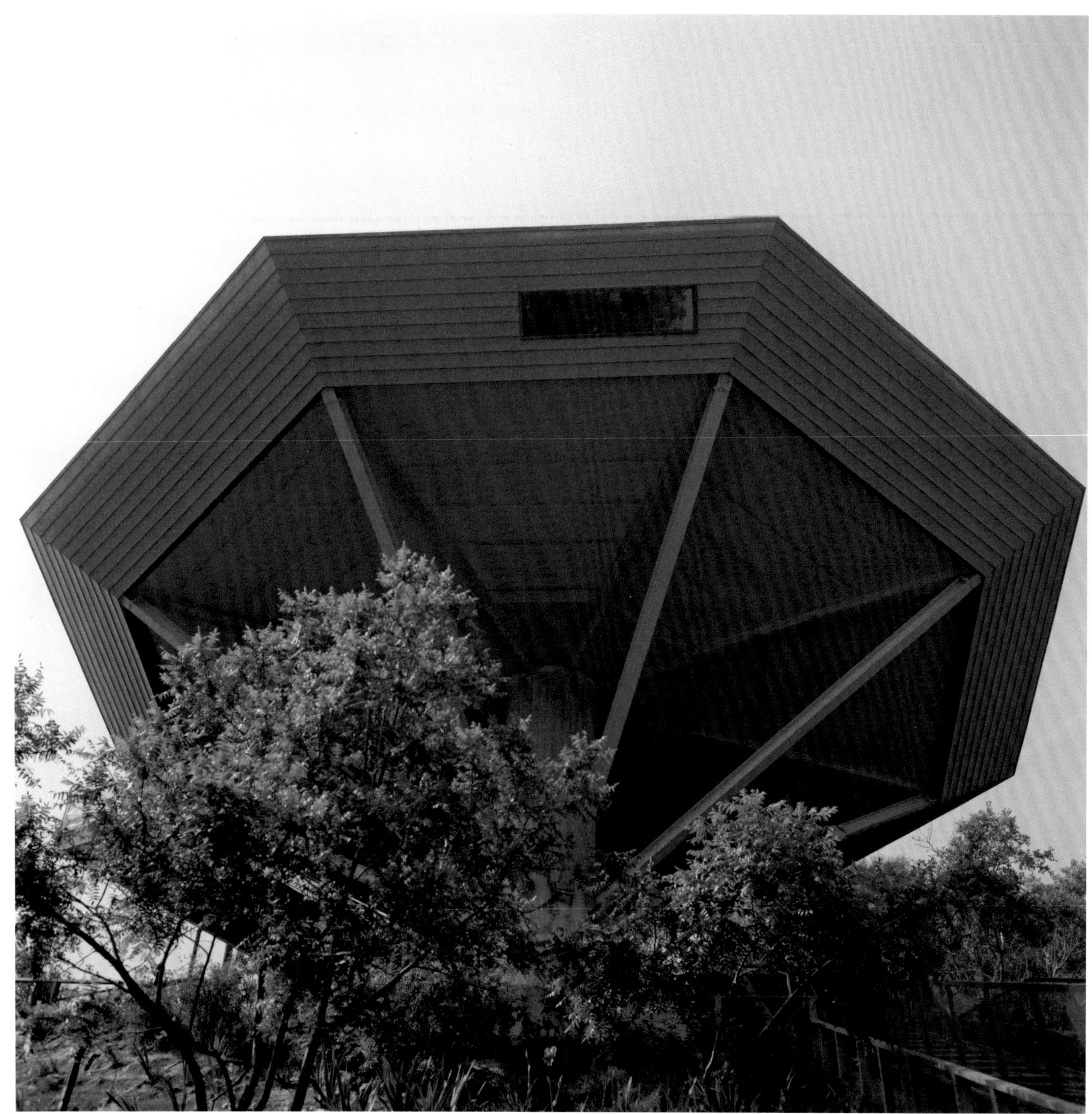

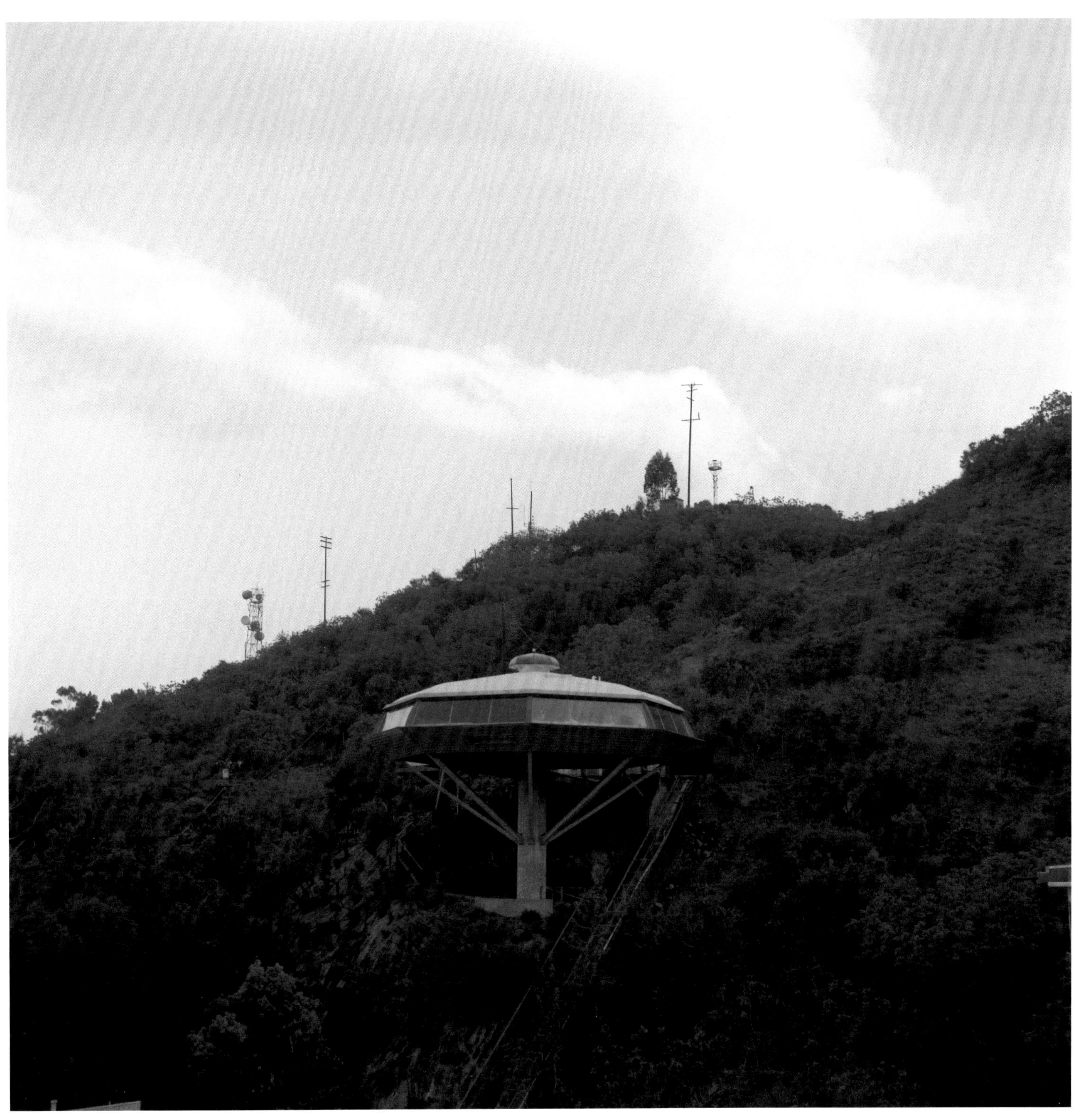

Chemosphere House
John Lautner, 1960 • Los Angeles, California

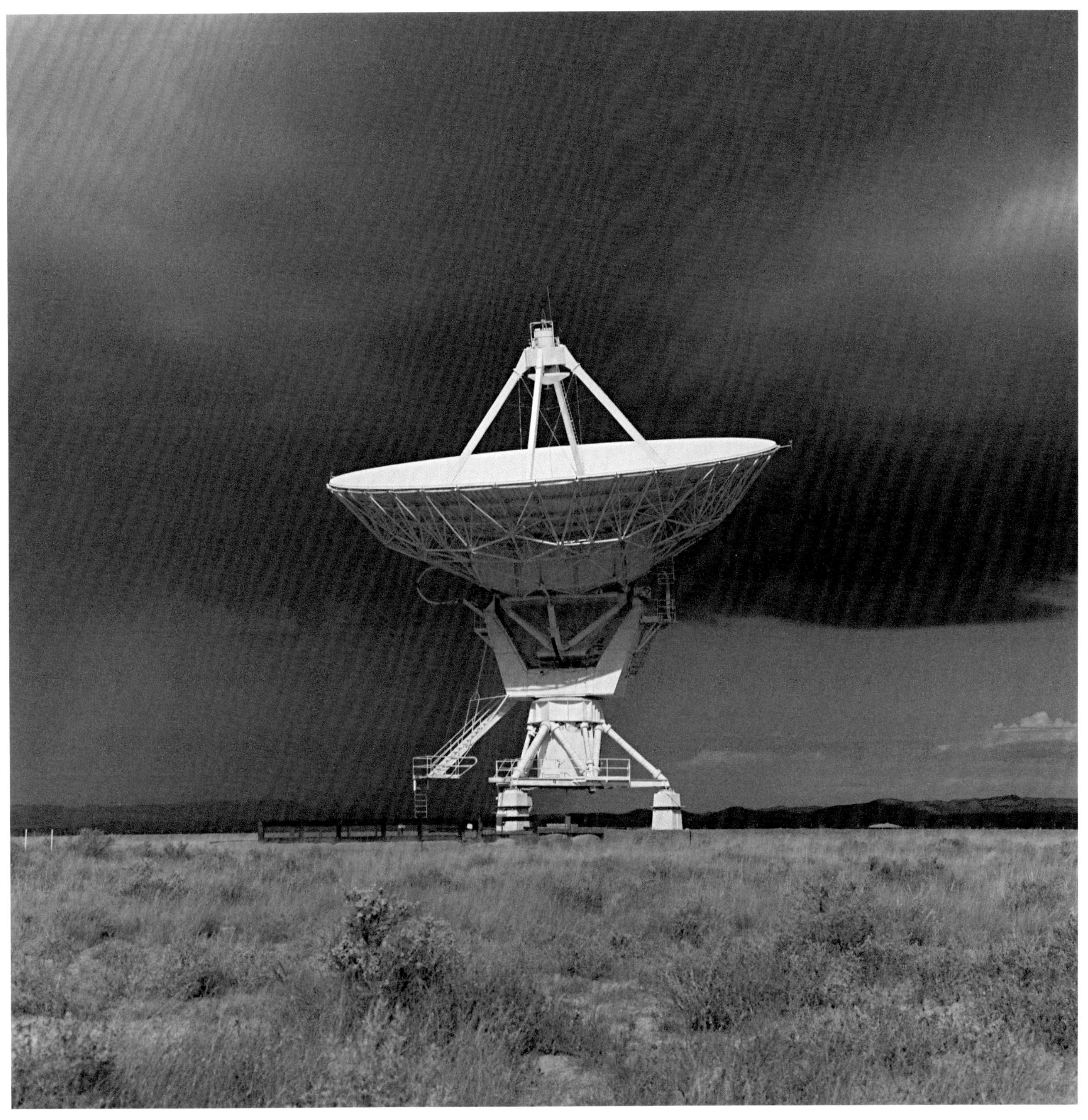

Very Large Array
1975–80 · *Plains of San Agustin, New Mexico*

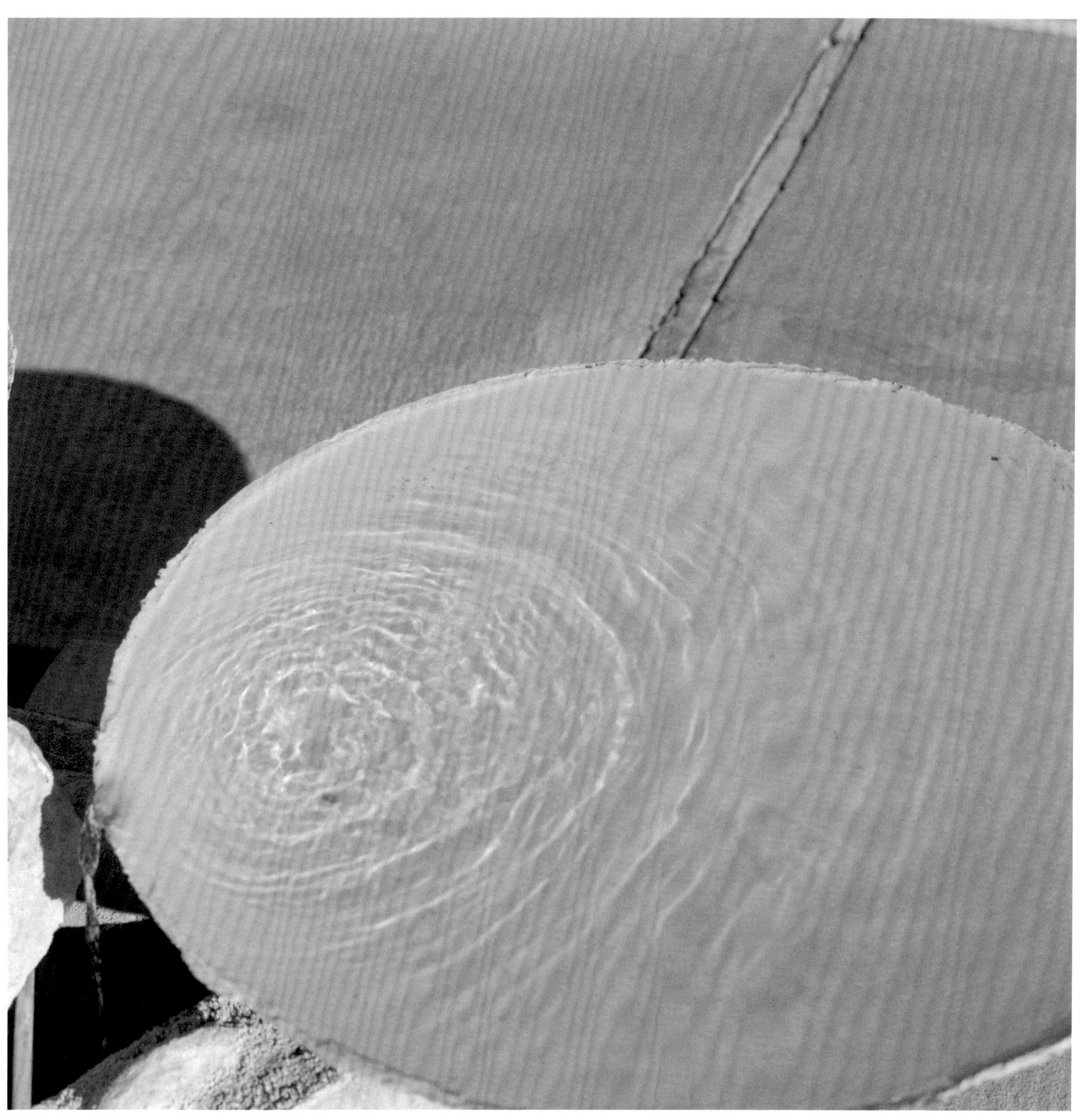

Fountain, Taliesin West
Frank Lloyd Wright, 1938 • Scottsdale, Arizona

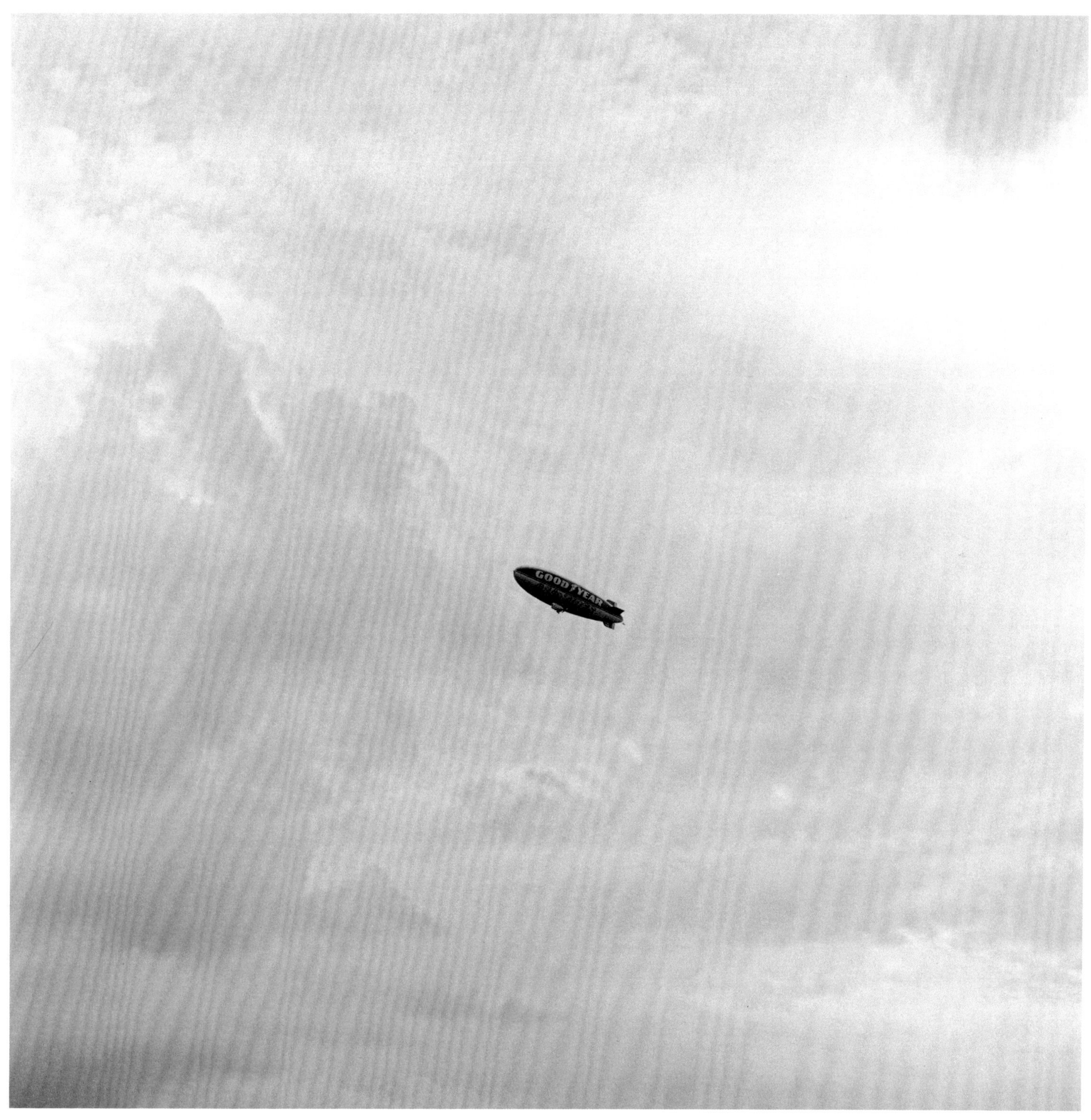

Goodyear Blimp
Above Texas

ACKNOWLEDGMENTS

To Brian McKee

To the Edwynn Houk Gallery: Edwynn Houk, Tanya Murray, Jenni Holder, Cheryl Pflanzer, John Cowey, and Susan Authur Whitson

To Hank's Photographic Services: Steve Rifkin, Brad Royce, Joe Hartwell, Simon Martinez, Marta Peterson, Mark Sage, Amanda Ortland, Eric Riha, and Sarah Hoffman

To The Monacelli Press: Gianfranco Monacelli, Andrea Monfried, and Evan Schoninger

To my studio manager, Chad Kleitsch, and assistant, Jessica Paulmann

To friends and family who helped on this project: Maxine Davis, David Boatwright, Helmet Horn, Steven Lowe, Jenee Misrahi, and Patti Sullivan

To Mark Holborn, for helping conceive the entire project

Last, to my husband, Rudy Wurlitzer, whose participation and enthusiasm for projects sends me on my way